Uniforms of the French Revolutionary Wars

Philip J. Haythornthwaite

Uniforms of the French Revolutionary Wars
1789-1802

Illustration by *Christopher Warner*

'*If I advance, follow me;*
if I retreat, shoot me;
if I am killed, avenge me!'

Henri de la Rochejacquelein

ARMS AND
ARMOUR

First published in 1981 by Blandford Press

This edition published Arms & Armour Press
A Cassell Imprint
Wellington House
125 Strand
London WC2R OBB

Copyright © 1997 Arms & Armour

Distributed in the United States by
Sterling Publishing Co Inc
387 Park Avenue South
New York, NY 10016-8810

British Library Cataloguing-in-Publication Data
A catalogue entry for this title is available from the British Library

ISBN 1-85409-445-9

Printed and bound in Hong Kong by
Dah Hua Printing Press Co

Contents

Introduction

Uniforms of the French Revolutionary Wars was first published by Blandford Press in 1981. In the present edition, the plates and text are reproduced unchanged, but the opportunity has been taken to provide an extended bibliography, including some of the relevant material which has appeared since the publication of the original edition. As in the original text, to facilitate initial further reading, some plate-references to volumes in the Blandford Colour Series are noted in the text to the plates.

The French Revolutionary Wars

Although the fall of the Bastille is generally regarded as the herald of the French Revolution, its roots lay deep in the social and economic history of France in the eighteenth century. The unrest amid French society in 1789 was a combination of bad harvests, a failing economy, weak administration and an ineffective monarch, an ever-growing socio-economic gulf between nobility and the rest, and debts from successive wars which had reduced the country to a shadow of its former strength. To a lesser degree, the unrest was compounded by egalitarian ideas from French philosophers and radicals like Tom Paine, and the experiences of Frenchmen who had witnessed, and aided, the American colonists' struggle for independence. A deteriorating economic climate and demands for reform from some aristocratic factions and the bourgeoisie (the 'Third Estate' amongst whom egalitarian philosophy was most prevalent) compelled King Louis XVI to convene the 'Estates General' in May 1789, the parliament last called in 1614.

Aided by the radical nobility, the 'Third Estate' secured the establishment of a National Assembly, which met to devise a constitution. Although the King acknowledged the change from absolute to constitutional monarchy, troop-concentrations in the suburbs of Paris led to a popular rising on 14 July 1789 which captured the Bastille prison, a hated symbol of despotism. Thereafter, events followed inexorably at a greater pace than ever envisaged by the moderate reformers. The King withdrew the troops (there was disaffection among the army), whereupon the aristocrats most opposed to the National Assembly, such as the Prince of Condé and Duke of Bourbon, made preparations to leave the country, the first trickle of 'émigrés' which soon became a torrent, depriving France of its trained and hereditary leadership.

Following the Bastille (at this stage its fall was hailed as a triumph by radical and even some conservative elements throughout Europe) came insurrection in the provinces, peasant uprisings destroying property and murdering or expelling their 'seigneurs'. Throughout France towns established elected assemblies and copied the formation of the 'National Guard' in Paris, a constitutional, and at this stage responsible, citizen-militia initially commanded by the Marquis de Lafayette, the popular hero of the American War and a champion of the National Assembly.

Provincial disorder forced the National Assembly to hurry through resolution after resolution on 4 August, destroying the feudal order and introducing equality of taxation; and on 26 August came the declaration of the Rights of Man, establishing a constitutional monarchy of which the King was titular head but with restricted power. The moderates were overtaken by events as fear of counter-revolution and famine caused further tumult; at the beginning of October a mob compelled the King and National Assembly to transfer from Versailles to Paris, where they were virtual prisoners under constant intimidation. Many moderates (the 'Right' of the Assembly) emigrated or stopped attending, leaving power with the radical 'Left', drifting ever leftwards. The symbols of revolution became common in the dress of adherents—the Phrygian cap or 'bonnet of liberty' and long trousers. These inspired the popular name for the revolutionaries: 'sans-culotte' (literally 'without breeches'). The address 'citoyen' ('citizen') replaced 'monsieur'. The 'Ancien Régime' was dead.

Political clubs had increasing effect, most notably the most extreme radicals, the Jacobins, self-appointed 'watch-dogs of the revolution'; the clergy was deprived of its religious prerogative and put upon a civil footing. Widespread discontent was aroused by the persecution of clergymen who refused to take the oath to the constitution, and Louis XVI (encouraged by his Queen, Marie Antoinette) tried to flee to the Marquis de Bouillé's army in the east which still had a vestige of discipline. Intercepted at Varennes, Louis was arrested and returned to Paris where, despite radical appeals for his trial, he was retained as powerless head of state.

Fears of the spread of revolutionary sentiments (initially to the Austrian Netherlands whose population would have welcomed French invasion), relentless agitation by émigrés, and Marie Antoinette's connection with the Austrian imperial family, made war almost inevitable. The Declaration of Pillnitz, made by Emperor Leopold II of Austria and King Frederick William II of Prussia in August 1791, stated that the restoration of the 'Ancien Régime' in France was the concern of every other sovereign and that they were prepared to act to this end. However, the initiative was taken, and war declared, by the new French Legislative Assembly.

The French army was ill-fitted for war, weakened in discipline and leadership by the emigration of officers. To supplement the hard core of old 'Royal' regular regiments, huge numbers of 'volunteers' (many conscripted) were formed into battalions in 1791–92; those based on the recently-disbanded provincial corps retained a trained cadre, but the remainder—particularly the battalions raised by the 'levée en masse' conscription of 1793—were largely worthless. Until the combination of regulars and recruits into the 'Amalgame' of 1794–95, the war was fought by a hotchpotch of reliable regulars and miscellaneous other formations of very mixed quality.

In 1792 war was presaged by an Austro-Prussian alliance, with Piedmont joining afterwards; France declared war and the Comte de Rochambeau's army marched on the Austrian Netherlands, where despite the weakness of the Austrian garrison the wretched French force was repelled. Disgusted by the conduct of his army, Rochambeau resigned and was replaced by Lafayette. The Duke of Brunswick, assembling an Austro-Prussian-émigré army at Coblenz, proclaimed his intention of marching on Paris and restoring the King; this caused yet more civil disturbances in Paris as a mob converged upon the Tuileries where Louis was guarded by the last vestige of his Household corps, the famed Swiss Guard, and a National Guard battalion. The latter either joined the mob or withdrew; the Swiss Guard resisted and was massacred. Lafayette's army refused to follow him to Paris to restore order and he fled to safety with the Austrians. In the wake of the slaughter at the Tuileries came the 'September massacres' in Paris, when 1,400 opponents of the Left were murdered, and there were similar (though less severe) purges in the provinces.

As Brunswick advanced lethargically upon Paris, Lafayette's successor, General Dumouriez, scrambled part of his 'Army of the North' to reinforce Kellermann's small

'Army of the Centre' opposing Brunswick. On 20 September 1792 Dumouriez and Kellermann concentrated 36,000 men to oppose 34,000 of Brunswick's 80,000 men at Valmy; fortunately for the French, the main bodies never engaged, Brunswick withdrawing after the first Prussian advance had been pushed back by a cannonade from artillery of the old Royal army.

Elsewhere, French success was more obvious: Savoy and Nice were captured, and from Alsace General Custine invaded Germany as far as Frankfurt. Meanwhile, the newly-elected National Convention had abolished the monarchy and declared a republic, their desire for a new beginning being so extreme that even the calendar was altered, 1792 becoming 'An 1' (Year One). Dumouriez, pushing into Flanders, followed the retiring Austrians and overwhelmed an outnumbered force at Jemappes (6 November); Brussels fell ten days later and Antwerp was threatened, arousing fears in Britain, hitherto a disinterested spectator. The year ended with Brunswick driving Custine back to the Rhine.

So far republican France was holding its own against the Austro-Prussian forces, but they doubled their own problems: firstly, in November 1792 the Convention declared support for all nations striving to repeat the events in France, mistakenly thinking that reformers in other countries were necessarily revolutionaries and would therefore support a French invasion; this 'crusade' panicked the other monarchies of Europe and made the extension of the war inevitable. Secondly, after a show trial, the ruling (though minority) Jacobin party led by Danton and Robespierre caused Louis XVI to be guillotined for treason in January 1793. In the next month France declared war on Britain, Spain and Holland, and shortly after was opposed by new members of the 'First Coalition' against her: Portugal, Naples and Tuscany.

The Allies attacked with two armies, those of the Prince of Saxe-Coburg (to recover the Austrian Netherlands), and Brunswick. On 18 March Dumouriez was soundly defeated by Saxe-Coburg at Neerwinden and, falsely accused of treason, fled to the allies like Lafayette before him. His replacement, General Dampierre, was killed near Condé in a vain attempt to stop Saxe-Coburg; Custine assumed command of the demoralized 'Army of the North', was defeated near Valenciennes (21–23 May 1793) and as a result was beheaded on the order of the 'Committee of Public Safety', a nine-member provisional government with absolute power, established by the Convention. Henceforth the shadow of the guillotine threatened every French general, each command being accompanied by 'Représentants du Peuple en Mission', sinister political commissars spying and interfering on behalf of the Committee of Public Safety.

As the Army of the North (now commanded by General Houchard) fled before the allies, 'The Terror' began in Paris. This was the judicial murder of political opponents, royalists, intellectuals, in fact anyone who posed a threat, real or imagined, to the radical minority headed by Robespierre, the virtual dictator. Over 1,200 victims were executed in Paris, including Marie Antoinette. Mass murder was also perpetrated in the provinces, particularly the Vendée and Brittany, both of which saw massive royalist counter-revolutions in 1793–94. In the Vendée, royalist gentry and middle-class leaders, like Henri de la Rochejaquelin, Cathelineau, Stofflet, Lescure and Charette de la Contrie, defeated successive republican forces with ill-disciplined, untrained peasant guerrillas, until extinguished by overpowering numbers and lack of matériel; in

3

Brittany the 'Chouan' revolt of Cottereau was suppressed with equal savagery. After the defeat of the royalist 'Grande Armée Catholique et Royale' in January 1794, a series of massacres and acts of incendiarism ('vengeance nationale') were carried out by the republican 'colonnes infernales' in these areas.

By Autumn 1793 France was on the verge of collapse: with civil war and atrocity inside and invaders pouring over the frontier. An Anglo-Hanoverian army under the Duke of York invested Dunkirk, linked to the Austrian by the Prince of Orange's Dutch army; an Anglo-Spanish fleet moved on Toulon, which declared for the monarchy in August. On 23 August the 'levée en masse' was instituted in France, conscripting the entire male population; though untrained, the republicans henceforth had superiority in numbers. The value of this was shown on 6 September when Houchard's 42,000 conscripts pushed back the Duke of York's 13,000 at Hondschoote, and a week later routed the Prince of Orange at Menin. In spite of this Houchard was guillotined in a purge, his replacement being General Jourdan.

The French army was meanwhile being transformed as war minister Lazare Carnot reorganized the remnants of the royal army and the hitherto useless levies, infusing a spirit of patriotism which turned the undisciplined mass attack into a formidable force. Carnot built the prototype of Napoleon's superlative army and encouraged reliance on manoeuvre instead of the more static tactics of the eighteenth century, to the extent that he became known as the 'Organiser of Victory'. And victories followed: on 15–16 October Jourdan defeated Saxe-Coburg at Wattignies; General Hoche in Alsace and on the Rhine, despite a check at Kaiserslautern (28–30 November), defeated Brunswick's Prussians at Fröschwiller (22 December) and Würmser's Austrians at Geisberg (26 December), so that by the year-end the invaders were back on their own side of the Rhine. Thanks to a plan of Colonel Napoleon Bonaparte, Toulon was recaptured on 19 December, and fighting on the Spanish frontier (despite widespread support for the Spanish among the French peasantry) resulted in 1794 with the inept Spanish being chased back as far as the Ebro.

Scenting victory, Carnot planned to clear French territory of invaders in 1794, his plan proving superior to the 'plan of annihilation' proposed by Austrian chief-of-staff Mack von Leiberich. Saxe-Coburg's Austro-Anglo-Hanoverians were defeated at Tourcoing (18 May), a drawn battle was fought at Tournai five days later, and at Hooglede (17 June) Allied victory was turned to defeat by a French counter-attack. Jourdan, now commanding the 'Army of the Sambre and Meuse' (a concentration of parts of three previous forces), invested Charleroi; unaware of its capture, Saxe-Coburg moved to its relief and was defeated at Fleurus (26 June), victim of another vigorous counter-attack which saved the French. Jourdan's victory was largely due to the spirit of the ordinary French soldiers, who called to their leaders: 'No retreat today!'

'The Terror' now reached its climax: in May 1794 Christianity was abolished in favour of 'The Cult of Reason', and severe Jacobin policies finally caused the revolt of the remainder of the National Convention, the execution of Robespierre and his adherents, abolition of the 'revolutionary tribunal' which had been responsible for the condemnation of 'traitors' and the resulting atrocities, the outlawing of political clubs and, particularly in the provinces, the 'White Terror' of the royalists avenging the excesses of the republicans.

Following Fleurus, the French occupied Brussels and Antwerp; General Moreau's 'Army of the Rhine and Moselle' advanced to besiege Mainz; General Pichegru invaded Holland; and the Allies were expelled from Savoy. Naval operations in 1794 centred on the Battle of the 1st of June, when British Admiral Lord Howe tried to intercept a French supply-convoy en route from the USA; though the French naval escort was defeated, the supply-ships reached their destination. In the West Indies, Sir John Jervis occupied Martinique, St Lucia and Guadeloupe, though these were later recovered by the French governor Hugues.

At the beginning of 1795 Pichegru completed his annexation of the Netherlands, his cavalry capturing the ice-bound Dutch fleet. Holland became the Batavian Republic, the first of several such satellites established by France. By the middle of the year hostilities between France and the exhausted Prussia were ended by the Treaty of Basle; Spain, Hanover, Saxony and Hesse-Cassel also made peace. A further triumph was the utter defeat of an émigré landing with British support at Quiberon, the émigrés (nominally part of the British army) being crushed by Hoche's waiting 'Army of the West'. Along the Rhine, Jourdan attempted an invasion of Germany in concert with Pichegru's 'Army of the Rhine and Moselle'; it failed because of Pichegru's involvement in a royalist plot. In Italy, General André Masséna came to prominence by a victory at Loano (23–5 November). A further Vendéan insurrection was extinguished brutally by Hoche before British reinforcements could disembark. Internally, dissolution of the National Convention and the establishment of a five-man government, the Directory, caused some unrest, including a royalist revolt in Paris, suppressed by General Bonaparte's artillery, gaining more prestige for the rapidly-rising young general.

Having secured the frontier, the French now changed gear into a war of expansion, partly to impose 'Liberty, Equality and Fraternity' by force (something of a contradiction), and partly to enable the enormous citizen armies to be fed. Carnot, now effectively chief of staff, planned a pincer movement against Austria, executed by the Armies of Sambre & Meuse and Rhone & Moselle striking through Germany, and the Army of Italy, uniting at Vienna. In Germany, the French commanders Jourdan and Moreau were opposed by Archduke Charles of Austria, whom Jourdan hoped to lure north to allow Moreau to invade Bavaria but, hampered by interference from the Directory, co-ordination was poor. Nevertheless, Jourdan's crossing of the Rhine and repulse at Wetzlar (16 June) allowed Moreau to advance and compelled Charles to divide his forces, both wings of which were driven back. Leaving General Latour to deal with Moreau, Charles switched to Jourdan and defeated him on 24 August at Amberg; but on the same day Moreau defeated Latour at Friedberg. Charles pressed after Jourdan, winning another brilliant victory at Würzburg on 3 September, after which Jourdan disengaged and fell back to the Rhine, where an armistice was signed. Learning of Jourdan's defeat, Moreau abandoned pursuit of Latour and withdrew.

In Italy, General Bonaparte assumed command of a wretched, starving and outnumbered French army in March 1796, 45,000 strong, stretching from Nice almost to Genoa. He was faced by two Allied armies: Baron Colli's Piedmontese and Beaulieu's Austrians, whose wide separation Bonaparte exploited. Striking between the two he widened the gap at Montenotte (12 April) and drove Beaulieu from Dego (14–15 April).

Instead of pursuing, Bonaparte turned on Colli, beat him at Mondovi (21 April) and forced an armistice which removed Piedmont from the war. Turning again on Beaulieu, Bonaparte outmanoeuvred him until he threatened Beaulieu's communications with the Austrian fortress of Mantua; and on 10 May Bonaparte defeated the Austrian rearguard at Lodi, personally leading a bayonet-charge across the town's bridge. More than simply compelling Beaulieu to continue his retreat, this enhanced Bonaparte's charismatic appeal to his men, perhaps the single most important reason for his later successes.

In seventeen days Bonaparte had conquered Lombardy, defeated two Allied armies, knocked Piedmont out of the war and added Savoy and Nice to French territory, but after a few days' rest he again advanced on Beaulieu, compelling the Austrians to continue their withdrawal, so that by the beginning of June all north Italy was in Bonaparte's hands, excepting the besieged Mantua. A new Austrian army, commanded by General Wurmser, hurried from the Tyrol, Wurmser himself making straight for Mantua whilst a smaller force under General Quasdanovich attempted to cut French communications. Bonaparte concentrated upon the latter column and destroyed it at Lonato (3 August), turned on Wurmser and beat him at Castiglione (5 August), then resumed the siege of Mantua as Wurmser fled back towards the Tyrol. Again, by interposing himself between two enemy armies, Bonaparte had beaten them in detail, a manoeuvre he exploited time and again throughout his career. Wurmser again divided his forces as he resumed the offensive, and was again defeated in detail, at Caliano (2 September) and Bassano (8 September), Wurmser taking refuge in Mantua whose garrison was thus swollen to 28,000. A third attempt to relieve Mantua met with more success initially—the French were checked at Caldiero (12 November), but a very hard-fought battle at Arcola (15–17 November) compelled Austrian general Baron Alvintzy to withdraw.

Operations in Germany in 1797 consisted of a renewed French advance, by Moreau and Hoche, the latter Jourdan's replacement in command of the 'Army of the Sambre and Meuse'. Without the skill of Archduke Charles, transferred to Italy, the Austrians were driven farther back, with one sizeable defeat in the Battle of the Lahn (18 April). Further operations on this front were forestalled by the events in Italy.

On 14 January Alvintzy attacked Bonaparte at Lodi; his initial success was ended by Masséna's arrival and the Austrians were driven from the field. A second Austrian force, trying to relieve Mantua, engaged the French besiegers but was surrounded and forced to surrender by Bonaparte's arrival; Wurmser's 16,000-strong garrison also surrendered on 2 February, having lost 18,000 men during the siege, mostly from disease. Reinforced, Bonaparte pushed into Austria itself, with Archduke Charles (having replaced Alvintzy) retiring before him. Masséna crushed an Austrian force at Malborghetto (10 March) and Bonaparte crossed the Alps with the intention of linking up with the armies marching from Germany; but Austria sued for peace, which was concluded by a preliminary treaty of 18 April, in which Bonaparte—without reference to the Directory—dictated his own terms, formalized by the Treaty of Campo Formio (17 October) by which the Austrian Netherlands became part of France and a further satellite, the Cisalpine Republic in north Italy, was recognized by Austria. The War of the First Coalition was ended with complete French victory, due to three factors: the patriotic fervour of the revolution, evidenced by the high spirit of the often barefoot and starving French soldiers; the organizational genius of Carnot; and the military genius of Bonaparte, whose audacious strategy completely baffled opposing commanders firmly rooted in the eighteenth century.

Other operations in 1797 were largely a result of Spain's defection from the Allies to France, by the Treaty of San Ildefonso (19 August 1796). The resulting threat caused Britain to evacuate Corsica and Elba; Admiral Jervis' British Mediterranean fleet cut off an attempt by the Spanish fleet to join that of France for an invasion of England, the Spanish fleet being smashed in the Battle of Cape St Vincent (14 February 1797), thanks to the impromptu manoeuvre of the commander of HMS *Captain*, Horatio Nelson. A small British expedition went to Portugal to forestall a possible Spanish invasion, but was never engaged. After mutinies among the British fleets at Spithead and the Nore—suppressed with little violence and resulting in a marked improvement in the conditions of service of the ordinary sailor—Admiral Duncan defeated the Dutch fleet at Camperdown (11 October). 1797 also saw a 'coup d'état' in France which turned the Directory into a dictatorship under Barras, depending for its existence upon the support of Bonaparte and the army. Political opponents—temporarily including Carnot, to whose efforts republican France owed its existence—were forced to flee the country.

Spring 1798 saw the establishment, by force, of two further French satellites: the Roman Republic (the old Papal States) and the Helvetian Republic in Switzerland. Bonaparte was placed in command of the 'Army of England', assembling at Dunkirk for a proposed invasion; but, doubtful of its chance of ever getting across the Channel in the face of the British Navy, he persuaded the Directory to transfer their attentions to Egypt, an outlet to the Orient and a base from which to attack the British in India. Consequently, in April he was given command of the 'Army of the Orient' which sailed in May, capturing Malta en route and landing in Egypt at the beginning of July. The Directory, no doubt, were pleased to have the dynamic and popular young general at sufficient distance not to pose any immediate political threat.

Bonaparte's 40,000 men stormed Alexandria on 2 July, defeating an Egyptian/Turkish force of 60,000 under Murad and Ibrahim in the 'Battle of the Pyramids' near Gizeh (21 July). On the next day the French occupied Cairo and began pursuit of Ibrahim towards Syria, but Bonaparte's entire plan was ruined on 1 August when Admiral Nelson's British fleet, sent to aid the Turks, completely annihilated the French fleet at the Battle of Aboukir Bay. Bonaparte was thus isolated from escape or reinforcement in a hostile land; a Turkish army under Achmed Pasha 'the Butcher' was forming in Syria, and another at Rhodes to invade Egypt with British assistance.

The other main centre of action in 1798 was Ireland, where years of unrest had been encouraged by radical nationalist societies like the 'United Irishmen'. Bitterness grew as loyalists and nationalists conducted an undeclared war against each other, until in 1798 the United Irishmen rose in revolt. The ill-equipped Irish peasant army with unskilled leaders (mostly peasants and priests) scored several successes against the equally inexperienced but less determined Irish loyalist militia. The rebellion was crushed with great brutality on either side, the most decisive rebel defeat being at Vinegar Hill (12 June). The French assistance, needed so desperately by the rebels, finally arrived in August, General Humbert's 1,200 men landing at Killala Bay and surrendering without a fight on 8 September, almost as big a fiasco as the abortive French 'invasion' of Pembrokeshire in February 1797.

At the end of 1798 the 'Second Coalition' was organized—Russia, Britain, Austria, Portugal, Naples, the Ottoman Empire and the Vatican. The French general Joubert overran Piedmont, and in November a Neapolitan army, commanded by the Austrian Mack von Leiberich, stormed into Rome, only to be driven out. The Allied strategy intended the Duke of York's Anglo-Russian army to recapture the Netherlands, Archduke Charles' Austrians to expel the French from Germany and Switzerland, and an Austro-Russian army under the ancient Russian general Suvarov to clear Italy, involving altogether some 300,000 Allied troops, plus Mack's 60,000 unreliable Neapolitans. To face them, the French had only about 210,000 (Jourdan's 46,000 on the upper Rhine, Masséna's 30,000 in Switzerland, 24,000 in Holland, 80,000 in north and 30,000 in south Italy), but nevertheless they went on to the offensive.

Initially, there was French triumph as Mack fled to the French to save his life from his mutinous Neapolitans, Naples was overrun and the Parthenopean Republic established. Farther north, however, French general Scherer tried to defeat Kray's Austrians before Suvarov arrived, but was himself defeated at Magnano (5 April). Suvarov, having arrived and defeated Scherer's successor, Moreau, at Cassano (27 April), by mid-June was caught by two French armies, Moreau and (marching from the south) General Macdonald. Suvarov faced Macdonald and defeated him at the Battle of the Trebbia (17–19 June), though Macdonald managed to link up with Moreau. As Suvarov pushed the French back to the Riviera, Moreau's successor, General Joubert, attacked Suvarov but was defeated and killed at Novi (15 August). Suvarov's pursuit was halted by news that General Championnet's French 'Army of the Alps' had entered Italy, but before he could tackle that too he was ordered to Switzerland with 20,000 Russians, leaving Marshal Melas' 60,000 Austrians to deal with Championnet, which he did at Genoa (4 November). By the end of the year almost all Bonaparte's gains had been erased by the redoubtable old Suvarov.

France fared better in Germany and the Netherlands. In March 1799 Jourdan's 'Army of Mayence' crossed the Rhine and attacked Archduke Charles' Austrians, twice as strong as the French; checked at Ostrach (21 March) Jourdan almost defeated the Austrians at Stockach (25 March), Austrian reinforcements winning the day, a Pyrrhic victory but one which wrecked the French advance. Jourdan resigned and was replaced by Masséna, but for the remainder of the year operations centred on the Netherlands and Switzerland.

In Holland the Duke of York's Anglo-Russian army met General Brune's Franco-Batavians in the first Battle of Bergen (16 September) and was defeated by lack of co-ordination between British and Russian elements. York advanced again and routed the opposition in the second Battle of Bergen (2 October), but lack of liaison again resulted in a check, at Castricum (6 October). Realizing that he had insufficient forces to recover the Netherlands, and as he had eliminated the Dutch fleet, York withdrew and hostilities ended with the convention of Alkmaar (18 October).

As the year began, Masséna advanced across the upper Rhine from Switzerland, in May taking command of a new formation, the 'Army of the Danube', comprising his

8

own forces plus Jourdan's defeated troops; he then withdrew towards Zurich (where he repulsed an Austrian attack on 4 June), and then farther westwards. Resuming the initiative, he was repulsed at Zurich (14 August). By this time a new Allied plan had been formulated, Charles to advance through western Germany to join York while Suvarov would march into Switzerland from Italy; however, Charles' departure left less than 40,000 Allied troops in Switzerland, and before Suvarov arrived Masséna routed Korsakov's Allied army in the third Battle of Zurich (25 September). This disaster caused Charles to abandon his march to the Netherlands and Suvarov, also retiring, was unfairly relieved of his command by the mad Czar Paul, an ignominious end to the old soldier's glorious career.

The campaigns in Europe in 1799 were disappointing for both sides; the French had lost Italy and the Allies wasted an opportunity of victory, and Russia withdrew from the war in disgust. The result might have been very different, however, had Bonaparte not been marooned in Egypt. Despite his unpromising position, he took the offensive in January 1799, marching into Syria with only 8,000 men; only the city of Acre, defended by British naval captain Sydney Smith, held out against Bonaparte. Achmed 'the Butcher' attempted to relieve Acre but was driven across the Jordan after the Battle of Mount Tabor (17 April); but despite this success Bonaparte abandoned the siege after plague had broken out among his troops, and returned to Cairo in June. In July the Turkish force from Rhodes landed and entrenched at Aboukir, 18,000 strong, but they were annihilated when Bonaparte attacked with only 6,000 men.

Realizing that the situation was stabilized and that further conquest was unlikely without reinforcement, and alarmed at the situation in Europe, Bonaparte turned over command to General Kléber and returned to France in a frigate. Within weeks he made himself absolute ruler of France, dissolving the Directory with the aid of his brother Lucien and the backing of the army. A 'Consulate' was established, a triumvirate in which the 'First Consul' was virtual dictator, an oligarchy disguised in democratic wrapping. Bonaparte, himself 'First Consul', eventually controlled a monarchy even more absolute than that of Louis XVI; a meteoric rise in six years from the simple artilleryman of Toulon.

An offshoot of the Revolutionary Wars in 1799 was the Fourth Mysore War, a continuation of a series of hostilities in India between the British East India Company and the native princes. The Third Mysore War (1789–92) had ended with Tippoo Sahib of Mysore accepting severe terms from the British; now Governor General Wellesley was ordered to extinguish the last sparks of French influence in Mysore lest Bonaparte should invade. Tippoo, secretly corresponding with France, resisted and was killed in the defence of Seringapatam as the war drew to a close. In this war a new British commander asserted himself, the Governor General's brother, Arthur Wellesley—later Duke of Wellington.

Despite Russia's withdrawal, the European war continued in 1800. The Austrians planned for General Kray to hold Germany secure, whilst Melas overwhelmed Masséna on the Riviera coast of Italy. Bonaparte organized a new 'Army of Reserve' at Dijon, planning to trap Melas between himself and Masséna, but in April Masséna's army was scattered and the General himself driven into Genoa. Bonaparte hurried to his aid, crossing the Great St Bernard pass, but Masséna capitulated after a gruelling siege (4

June). Melas, in Turin, discovered Bonaparte cutting his communications with Austria and immediately moved east, the Austrian force marching from Genoa being defeated by General Lannes' French corps at Montebello (9 June). Bonaparte, believing Melas to be in Turin, had his army widely dispersed when he ran into serious opposition at Marengo (14 June). With only 18,000 men he was driven back two miles and Melas, thinking himself victorious, continued his march east. But Bonaparte rallied his troops and, reinforced, counter-attacked in the late afternoon and shattered Melas' army so completely that the Austrian capitulated next day. Bonaparte had luckily emerged victorious from his second Italian campaign.

On the other front, Moreau drove Kray into Bavaria, winning victories at Stockach (3 May), Möskirch (5 May), Ulm (16 May) and Hochstadt (19 June); in July an armistice was arranged, ending in November, by which time Kray had been replaced by the youthful Archduke John. He clashed with Moreau at Hohenlinden (3 December) and was utterly crushed. Moreau marched towards Vienna as Macdonald's French army invaded the Tyrol from Switzerland and General Brune, now commanding Bonaparte's forces in Italy, advanced towards the passes in the Julian Alps. On Christmas Day Austria sued for peace.

In Egypt in 1800, Kléber agreed to evacuate his army in return for a guaranteed free passage to France. Britain disavowed the agreement and Kléber resumed the offensive, defeating a Turkish army at Heliopolis (20 March); but on the day of Marengo he was assassinated and General Menou assumed command of the isolated French.

The series of savage slave revolts and native rebellions in the West Indies culminated with the restoration of order in Haiti in 1800, after ten years of chaos. A Negro commander, Toussaint L'Ouverture, established peace, but prompted Bonaparte to attempt the re-establishment of French dominance over the island; a vicious guerrilla war between Toussaint and General Leclerc's 25,000-strong French expedition continued until Toussaint was treacherously seized during negotiations and imprisoned in France (where he died in 1803); his successor, Dessalines, renewed the war until the demoralized French withdrew in 1803 after Leclerc had died of fever. Elsewhere, the West Indies swallowed whole armies of Europeans as successive garrisons were wiped out by disease; for example from 1794 to 1797 80,000 British troops (including many émigrés enlisted to fight for the restoration of the French monarchy) died or were permanently disabled, almost all from sickness.

1801 saw no hostilities on land in Europe, the Treaty of Lunéville (9 February) re-affirming Campo Formio. Russia, Prussia, Denmark and Sweden formed a league of 'armed neutrality' to protect their shipping from British incursions; Britain's response was to send Admiral Sir Hyde Parker to the Baltic. Parker's subordinate, Horatio Nelson, disregarded his orders and sailed into Copenhagen harbour on 2 April and smashed the Danish fleet; he hoped to deal with the Russian fleet the same way, but hostilities were ended by the assassination of the Czar and an armistice. Two other naval actions of 1801 were fought by British Admiral Saumarez at Algeciras; the first an inconclusive engagement against the French (6 July), and the second a victory against a Franco-Spanish fleet six days later.

In Egypt, an Anglo-Turkish army under Sir Ralph Abercromby landed at Aboukir (8 March 1801), defeating Menou on 20 March, though Abercromby was killed.

The Allies pushed on, taking Cairo and Alexandria, until the isolated Menou capitulated (31 August), his army being granted free passage to France. British sea power had finally destroyed Bonaparte's dream of oriental conquest.

The French Revolutionary Wars ended at the Peace of Amiens in March 1802, bringing peace to Europe for the first time in a decade. On 2 August 1802 Bonaparte was proclaimed 'Consul for Life', a short step from his coronation in December 1804 as Emperor of the French, founding a dynasty which was to last only a decade. Peace lasted but a year, before the 'Third Coalition' took the field against France.

The period from 1789 to 1802 saw a dramatic change in the political structure of Europe. It was not simply that one ruling power (the French monarchy) had been supplanted by another: the major change was in the idea of the sovereignty of the people, exemplified by the supposedly democratic character of republican France and her citizen-armies which, at least initially, were imbued with a missionary zeal not only to defend their own territory—'theirs' in the sense of belonging to them rather than to a feudal overlord—but to spread the gospel of 'Liberté, Égalité, Fraternité' to the other 'subject' peoples of Europe. The latter desire is what alarmed the rulers of other states; the idea of restoring the French monarchy for its own sake was small motive for a declaration of war upon republican France. It could be argued that the success of the Revolution paved the road for the democracy and national independence of the later nineteenth century, but at a horrific price in spilled blood even up to 1802, though the worst carnage was still to come in the future campaigns of the new Emperor Napoleon. In France and her satellites the Revolution and the wars which followed had the effect, via an inordinate amount of human suffering, of replacing one autocracy with another, with an interval of strife-ridden, supposed 'freedom' between the two.

Armies of the French Revolutionary Wars

There is insufficient space for any detailed analysis of the composition and comparison of the various national armies involved in the Revolutionary Wars; indeed, certain aspects have already been covered in previous titles of the Blandford Colour list. However, some factors peculiar to this part of the Napoleonic conflict should be examined, as they have implications concerning the tactics and strategy of the period.

Throughout the eighteenth century, 'manoeuvre' had played an increasingly important rôle, as opposed to static tactics in which blocks of troops battered each other until one gave way. Rapid manoeuvre, however, necessitated the close formation of units into small, dense masses or 'columns', in which only the first two or three ranks could fire their muskets. In general, commanders were unwilling to sacrifice the 'firepower' of a three- or four-deep line, in which at least three-quarters of the men could fire their muskets, for the sake of additional mobility.

A radical change in the reliance upon 'line' evolved basically out of necessity, by the rapid expansion of the French army at the beginning of the Revolutionary Wars. In 1789 each of the French regular infantry regiments had two battalions (the 28th had four); these were the backbone of French resistance in the very first campaigns, even though their quality had deteriorated over the previous few decades. Despite mutinies and the emigration of many officers and some other ranks, however, their innate discipline enabled them to fight in the classic manner, the complex drill and textbook manoeuvre which demanded extensive training.

The newly-raised regiments were very different. In March 1791 the old provincial troops were disbanded and replaced by the untrained National Guard, raised for political reasons and of little military value. Later in the same year the Assembly raised 169 new volunteer battalions, organized by the provinces, of reasonable calibre as they included members of the disbanded provincial corps. In 1792 another contingent of 'volunteer' battalions was raised, the men unwilling recruits conscripted by ballot, of very low quality. Equally bad was the levy of 20,000 'Féderés' sent to Paris in 1792; one such battalion was implicated in the Tuileries massacre. Even worse were the thousands of conscripts swept up by the 'levée en masse' in 1793, many unwilling, many deserting, and the remainder ill-equipped, untrained and wretchedly disciplined.

The two component sections of the French army were nicknamed from the colour of their uniform: 'les blancs', the regulars of the old army who retained the white coat, and 'les bleus', the blue-coated volunteers and conscripts. Detaille's drawing 'Les Blancs et Les Bleus', though not contemporary, aptly illustrates the respective merits of the two: the white-coated regulars calmly stand firm whilst the blue-coated rabble flee in confusion.

The French army began the Revolutionary Wars with the manoeuvres recommended by the 1791 Drill-Book, the product of the last years of the 'Ancien Régime', which advised a rapid advance in column until contact with the enemy, when the column should deploy into line and utilize maximum firepower. But the untrained 'bleus' had no concept of orderly manoeuvre and chaos ensued. After the first defeats a new tactic had to be evolved to utilize the few assets of the conscripts: first weakening the enemy with artillery and skirmish-fire performed by the most reliable men, the remainder would make a bull-headed rush towards the enemy in a disorderly mob, carried forward on a tide of patriotism, until beaten back or until they burst through the enemy line, in either case horrifically expensive. General Foy has left a somewhat romanticized picture of such a charge:

'. . . an officer, common soldier, or, as often as not, a Representative of the People, would start to chant the "Hymn of Victory". The general would place his hat . . . on the point of his sword so that it could be seen from afar and serve as a rallying point for the gallant troops. The soldiers would begin to run forwards, those in the front ranks crossing their bayonets, as the drums beat the charge; the sky would ring to a thousand battle-cries constantly repeated: "En avant! En avant! Vive la République!"'

Often this mad rush would overwhelm an enemy bound by the staid tactics of the eighteenth century, but the undisciplined French mob could as easily run away, only 'les blancs' preserving a semblance of predictability in their movements.

The solution to the problem of creating a cohesive force of even quality was the 'Amalgame', first authorized in February 1793 but not activated until a year later. This ingenious scheme reorganized the entire army into 'demi-brigades' (the term 'regiment' being shunned for political reasons). Each regular regiment became the nucleus for two 'demi-brigades', each of which comprised three battalions, one regular and two 'volunteer' or conscript. Thus in December 1794 the 1st Btn of the old 1st Regt was joined with the 5th Paris and 4th Somme volunteers to form the new 2nd Demi-Brigade. The regular battalion invariably became the 2nd or 'centre' battalion of the demi-brigade, the tactical implication being obvious. In order to combine the two assets of the French army—regulars' firepower and the impetus of the volunteers' charge—the demi-brigade thus incorporated a battalion which could fight in line and provide firepower, and on each flank a battalion which could utilize the rapid advance.

This formation was so successful that it developed into the classic formation of Napoleonic warfare, 'l'ordre mixte', which operated at all levels from battalion to division, in which alternate units provided firepower whilst others delivered hammer-blows in column. Until the French eventually met an adversary whose firepower and tactical skill was equal, the system was potentially invincible.

There were two kinds of demi-brigade: 'demi-brigades de bataille' of 'line' infantry, and 'demi-brigades légères', formed around the old 'chasseur à pied' (light infantry) regiments. Initially there were 198 'de bataille' and fifteen 'légères', increasing to 211 and 32 respectively until in January 1796 the weaker demi-brigades were broken up amongst the 100 'de bataille' and thirty 'légères' which remained; for example the 2nd Demi-Brigade absorbed two battalions of the old 161st. This organization was retained until September 1803, when the term 'regiment' was re-introduced, and 'demi-brigade' relegated to a loosely-used term indicating provisional groupings of battalions. Strength naturally varied. Each battalion supposedly comprised nine companies, of which eight were designated 'fusiliers', plus (in the traditional way) one 'élite' company of grenadiers, in theory if not practice the battalion's bravest men; three companies would often be used as skirmishers to precede an attack. 'Demi-brigades légères' battalions comprised six companies, four of 'chasseurs' (equivalent to fusiliers), one of 'carabiniers' (grenadiers) and one of 'voltigeurs' (skirmishers). It was rare for a light demi-brigade to be more than 1,000 strong or a line demi-brigade 2,500, whatever the unit's official establishment.

The French cavalry suffered greatly from the emigration of officers and even whole regiments, and because of the time needed to train a proficient cavalryman the deficit was not made up for years. The ex-royal cavalry remained steady but the newly-raised regiments (1791–92) were more wretched than their infantry counterparts. As in all armies, the old army comprised heavy cavalry (26 regiments, including two of carabiniers), medium (eighteen regiments of dragoons), and light (six of hussars and twelve of 'chasseurs à cheval'). Establishment fluctuated, a cavalry demi-brigade usually comprising four squadrons of two companies each, with 116 men per company. The establishment of around 900 was rarely attained, two or three hundred being the average. Though the cavalry's triumphs were few in the Revolutionary Wars, the foundations were laid for the formidable and decisive force ultimately controlled by Napoleon.

The artillery was the best part of the Republican army, whose officers were largely middle-class and thus suffered least from the effects of emigration. Their weapons, thanks to Gribeauval's previous reforms, were the best in Europe, and though their transport depended upon the employment of unreliable civilians, their performance was outstanding—witness Valmy. An important innovation was 'artillerie volante', batteries in which all gunners were mounted and which moved even faster than ordinary horse artillery. The use of massed-battery fire (the concentration of numbers of cannon to bombard a specific sector of the enemy line), though not employed to the effect it had later, was nevertheless a potent weapon when the massing of batteries could be achieved, as at Castiglione and Marengo.

The very wretchedness of French equipment gave them an advantage in the speed of manoeuvre attainable as a result. By having little baggage, and, initially out of necessity, having to forage and scavenge for food instead of being supplied in the conventional way, meant that the French invariably were able to outmarch and outmanoeuvre any enemy who relied for provender upon organized transportation of supplies from depôt to army. Though it had its disadvantages—notably the necessity of keeping troops widespread so as not to exhaust an area too quickly—'living off the land' was a further vital factor in the successes gained by Napoleon in the early part of his Imperial reign.

By contrast, the armies opposing the French were universally hidebound in theory and manoeuvres of the eighteenth century, so that when they encountered the 'horde' tactics of the French they were insufficiently flexible to counter it; and thus could untrained French levies overthrow the better-disciplined, better-equipped, professional troops of other powers by the simple expedient of a headlong rush.

The emergence of light infantry as a potent force on the battlefield was another product of the Revolutionary Wars. The cloud of skirmishers was a feature of every French attack until the end of the Napoleonic Wars, but other nations were slow to emulate them. Britain had perfected light infantry tactics during the American War, but reactionary commanders insisted on the retention of archaic drill to such an extent that after the brief interval between wars British regimental light companies were so unskilled that German mercenaries had to be employed as light infantry in the early campaigns.

The use of foreign troops in national armies was another feature of the Revolutionary Wars. Various nations had employed mercenaries for years, but the habit reached a peak in the mid-1790s, largely due to the number of 'émigrés' who enlisted in foreign armies to assist the restoration of the French monarchy. Such troops, often including aristocrats and gentry serving as privates, were the best of the 'foreign' corps; at the other end of the scale were regiments formed by the recruitment of prisoners of war, a hazardous business at best which usually produced wretched units whose main aim was to desert to their own side as soon as possible. Britain recruited a number of such corps and sent them to the West Indies where the chance of desertion (and survival) was small. As the boundaries of France incorporated hitherto independent states, the French army became increasingly multi-national, particularly when the satellite states supplied whole armies. Frequently these troops were conscripted and thus were without the ardour of the patriotically-inspired French.

Uniforms of the French Revolutionary Wars

At the beginning of the Revolutionary Wars most armies dressed in a similar fashion, different in colour and ornaments but involving a natural progression from the long coats of the beginning of the eighteenth century. The coat, though still long-tailed, was swept back off the front of the legs by permanently-fixed 'turnbacks', a relic of the habit of disencumbering the legs of the long coat-'skirts' before action; the coat was no longer fastened across the breast, but usually cut with lapels which exposed the waistcoat from neck to waist. Breeches and stockings or gaiters were the usual wear, long trousers rarely being seen. The commonest hat, originally a 'tricorne', was evolving into a two-cornered felt construction with a slight 'peak' at the front as a relic of the third corner. Such was the impractical and uncomfortable costume of the ordinary infantry-man, made even worse by the high stock around the neck (a leather or fabric collar intended to keep the head erect) and tight leather belts.

Certain troops in all armies wore items of uniform associated with their rôle. Grenadiers, for example, wore mitre-shaped caps, with brass front-plates in Protestant countries and fur caps in Catholic countries and Britain; the 'fusiliers' of some German states had miniature grenadier-caps with smaller brass fronts. Heavy cavalry generally wore the cocked hat, coat and high boots; in Germanic armies their uniforms were often white, a relic of the buff-leather coats of the previous century. Hussars wore imitation Hungarian dress, with pelisse and tall cap. Light infantry wore what was supposed to be a functional, short-skirted uniform and small cap, as better befitted their skirmishing duty, though in effect their uniform was often as impractical as that of their pipe-clayed, hair-powdered mannikin comrades.

The Revolution changed that within months. Whereas the nucleus of French regular troops wore their old uniforms, the newly-raised battalions were given hastily-produced blue coats and ill-assorted legwear or, at least initially, wore half-military and half-civilian dress in varying degrees of verminous dilapidation. The red 'cap of liberty' and long trousers (often striped) were worn by military and civilians alike, while the leaders affected outrageous styles festooned with every trinket imaginable.

In many armies, the Revolutionary Wars saw the introduction of a new cap, inspired by the Austrian 'kaskett'. This head-dress, worn by Austria until 1798, was a low, cylindrical leather cap which, when provided with a peak, set the fashion for the next sixty years as the ubiquitous shako. As the shako appeared elsewhere, however, Austria replaced the 'kaskett' with a ponderous, imitation-classical, boiled-leather helmet. By the end of the Revolutionary Wars the shako had replaced, or was about to replace, the cocked hat. The other radical change in uniform concerned the coat, which was gradually replaced by a short-tailed jacket which fastened to the waist. Another style which had its genesis in the 1790s was 'Polish uniform' of square-topped cap ('czapka') and 'kurtka' or lancer-jacket, inspired by Polish émigrés; its real heyday, however, came in the Napoleonic Wars proper.

National styles are described in the text to individual plates, but mention must be made here of two factors which are not always remembered. Firstly, there was the impracticality of uniforms at the beginning of the Revolutionary Wars—helmets which fell off, hairstyles which took hours to fix, decorative coats which failed to keep the soldier warm. For example, the 'Inspection Returns' of British regiments make frequent mention of the hats, so small as to perch on top of the head and have to be tied on with ribbons, and 'functional' light infantry caps which fell off as easily, and which had no peak to shade the eyes of a soldier expected to aim at an individual target.

The second point concerns the general dilapidation of uniforms, particularly (but not exclusively) on campaign. The elegant head-dress might collapse around the ears in wet weather and clothes fall to pieces from the rigours of campaign, but some troops, particularly the French, took the field in an unbelievably wretched state to begin with, due to lack of resources. In the first campaigns probably more French troops were barefoot than had shoes, and a story exists whereby the Loire-Inférieure Battalion was given wooden 'sabots' (clogs) as a special reward for gallant conduct!

The drastic state of an army's clothing on campaign can be seen from the quantities of garments dispatched to the British army in Flanders in the winter of 1793–94 by the patriotic 'United Society'; for although much of the clothing subscribed was doubtless needed in addition to 'issue' clothing to combat the severity of the winter, some undoubtedly went to replace clothing worn out on campaign or which the troops had never been issued with (some had been rushed overseas wearing 'slop clothing', just linen jacket and trousers). Some items listed in contemporary reports must have gone to soldiers' wives and camp-followers, for among the items sent were 327 pairs of women's shoes, 98 shifts, 324 bed gowns, 462 petticoats and 84 women's cloaks. The more usual items included 28,000 waistcoats (the most urgent need), over 10,000 pairs of shoes and 15,000 caps, 903 pairs of 'trouzers' and 'a Bag of horse hair socks'. Colours were apparently immaterial, for records mention 'loose Blue Great Coats' and blue or brown trousers. Other bizarre items included woollen mittens and caps and, for troops in Toulon in 1794, '4,000 Woollen Caps and Welsh Wigs', the latter fluffy woollen caps with side- and neck-flaps like an old periwig!

The state of the army to which these supplies were sent is recorded by an anonymous diarist, quoted by Lawson: 'The want of necessary cloathing was now severely felt, as the cold began to grow intense. The officers in several regiments set on foot a subscription to furnish their men with a few comforts of life. The regimental cloathing being worn out, it was curious to see to what shifts some soldiers were put to keep themselves warm and comfortable. One would have on a large pair of Dutchman's wide breeches to his regimental jacket, another would have a large full brimmed Burgomaster's coat on by way of a surtout, and another to his red jacket would have sewed a pair of wide black or brown sleeves with long hanging cuffs; with other curious contrasts of cloathing—so that from the motley appearance . . . it would have been a difficult matter . . . to tell to what nation they belonged . . . it was no uncommon thing to see an officer with the skirts of his regimental coat cut off to repair the body of it, or to keep it whole at the elbows. . . .'

The armies of other states fared similarly, suffering from ill-designed uniforms, frequently of inferior quality due to unscrupulous manufacturers and regimental colonels. Thus the appearance presented by the soldier of the Revolutionary Wars often better befitted a ragged mob of scarecrows than an army.

The provision of personal equipment was affected not only by the rigours of campaign but by the ill-preparedness of most armies. As late as the Egyptian campaign it was customary for French soldiers to tie their greatcoat to the knapsack with string, there being no official provision of leather straps. Inexperience also had dire effects; for example, the diarist quoted above describes the British army's equipment on landing in Holland as: '. . . a blanket, a canteen or small wooden cask holding about three English pints, for the purpose of carrying water or spirits on the march, a haversack or linen bag, slung over the shoulder, for bread or provisions; these with knapsack, arms and accoutrements . . . there was not allowed to either officers or privates any kind of baggage . . . except what each carried for himself. . . .' The result of this excessive load was that '. . . to rid themselves of part of their burthen the contents of the knapsacks, as shoes, shirts, stockings, etc. were scattered along the road . . .' by the men.

Few lessons had been learned, for, as Surtees records, the British troops disembarking in the Helder campaign (1799) were ordered to carry only 'light marching order', about half the necessary equipment, the remainder being stored away in casks. Concerning his own regiment (56th), Surtees notes that no greatcoats had been provided, only blankets, with '. . . no proper . . . mode of carrying them', the blanket being *worn* in lieu of a coat: 'Some had their blankets thrown around them, others had them twisted up like a horse collar, and tied over their shoulders in the manner of a plaid. . . .' So inexperienced were these troops that many believed a rumour that they had been officially permitted to throw away their knapsacks if they were any encumbrance. Like Surtees, many of his regiment 'played the young soldier' to their great regret, having neither knapsack nor blanket for bivouac, even officers discarding their kit. One, says Surtees, unsuccessfully offered half a guinea for the use of a blanket for one night. For the remainder of the campaign they were compelled to carry everything in the haversack, an '. . . inconvenient bag, which, hanging so low as to knock against my thighs, greatly impeded my progress. . . .' One 'concession' to active service noted by Surtees is the use, in place of breeches and gaiters, of trousers, though due to the severe climate '. . . I have actually seen the water running out of the bottom of the men's trowsers like that from a gutter which carries the rain from the roof of a house . . .'. Despite his criticisms, Surtees witnessed with horror the men of the 35th trimming their own hair with knives by cutting off the 'queue', a most sensible practice on campaign, but a heinous 'breach of discipline, as I could not have anticipated; for though on the whole it was an improvement . . . yet . . . for a body of soldiers, without any permission from higher authority . . . to break . . . the custom of the service, was . . . an utter renunciation of all obedience to authority . . .'.

As armies became more experienced, instructions like the British General Order of 6 March 1801 were issued, ordering knapsacks to be left aboard ship by troops disembarking in Egypt, only the haversack and a rolled blanket slung across the back being carried; but such orders were only issued in those cases where the knapsack would have been a genuine encumbrance and its contents not vital for the soldier's well-being.

An additional consequence of insufficient provision of 'necessaries' in the field was to hasten the dilapidation of uniform; Surtees, for example, notes that having thrown away his equipment, his uniform rapidly became '. . . all filth and dirt; our arms the colour of our coats with rust; our faces as black as if we had come out of a coal-pit . . . we cut the most ludicrous figure imaginable . . . most sorry figures, being literally nothing but rags and dirt . . .'. Surtees might have been describing the appearance of the soldier of the French Revolutionary Wars in general.

Colour Plates

1 a) 'Sans-Culotte', 1792.
  b) Private, Gardes Suisses, 1792.

FRANCE

2 a) Trooper, Hussards de Chamborant, 1789–90.
  b) Grenadier, 23rd Regt, 1789 (Régt du Roi).

3 a) Fusilier, 42nd Line, 1791.
   b) Fusilier Lieutenant, 32nd Line, 1792.

FRANCE

4 Officer with Colour, 7th Btn,
  5th Div., Paris National
  Guard (District des Blancs-
  Manteaux), 1790.

5 a) Private, 6th Infantry Regt (Guard Grenadiers), 1789.
  b) Officer, Garde du Corps, 1790.
  c) Trooper, 2nd (von Beeren) Cuirassiers, 1790.

PRUSSIA

6 a) Adjutant General of Cavalry, 1790.
   b) Trooper, 10th Hussars, 1791.

7 a) Trooper, 9th Hussars, 1791.
   b) N.C.O., 3rd Hussars, 1791.

8 a) Sergeant, Battalion Company, 2nd Foot Guards, 1792.
b) Officer, Battalion Company, 2nd Foot Guards, 1792.
c) Grenadier, 2nd Foot Guards, 1792.

9 a) Officer, 1st Foot, 1794.
   b) Private, Grenadier Company, 36th Foot, 1791.
   c) Sergeant, Grenadier Company, 36th Foot, 1791.

HANOVER

10 a) Officer, 3rd Cavalry, 1790.
    b) Private, 14th Light Infantry, 1794.

11 a) Pontooneer, 1790.
    b) Sapper, 1790.
    c) Driver, Train, 1790.

BADEN/SAXONY

12 a) Baden: Trooper, Garde du Corps, 1790.
    b) Saxony: Trooper, Kurfürst Cuirassiers, 1785.

13 a) Fusilier, 11th Regt, 1790.
   b) Fusilier Corporal, 5th Regt, 1790.

BAVARIA

14 a) Trooper, Chevauleger Regt Fugger, 1792.
    b) Trooper, Minucci Cuirassiers, 1792.

15 a) Fusilier, 42nd Regt, 1792.
    b) Dragoon, campaign dress, 1789.
    c) Officer, Wurmser's Friekorps, 1793.

FRANCE

16 Infantry privates, 1793.

17 a) Trooper, Hussards de la Morte, 1793.
    b) Officer, Hussards de la Liberté, 1792.
    c) Trooper, 4th Hussars, 1799.

FRANCE

18 a) Private, Volontaires de Santerre.
   b) Officer, Vendéan rebels (Marquis de Lescure).
   c) Vendéan infantryman.

19 a) Officer, Artillery, 1792.
    b) Private, Légion des Allobroges, 1792.

FRANCE

20 a) Veteran, Paris National Guard, 1790.
    b) Student, École de Mars, 1794.
    c) Lady 'pikeman', 1794.

21 a) Officer, Royal Artillery, campaign dress, 1794.
    b) Civilian driver, Royal Artillery, 1793.
    c) Gunner, Royal Artillery, 1792.

BRITAIN

22 a) Officer, 2nd Dragoon Guards, 1797.
    b) Officer, 3rd Dragoon Guards, 1790.

23 a) Sergeant, 10th Light Dragoons, 1793.
   b) Trumpeter, 10th Light Dragoons, dismounted dress, 1793.

BRITAIN

24 a) Drummer, Buckinghamshire Militia, 1793.
   b) Grenadier, Buckinghamshire Militia, 1793.

25 a) Sergeant Major, Royal Edinburgh Volunteers, 1795.
    b) Officer, Royal Huddersfield Fusiliers, 1796.

26 a) Switzerland: Commandant, Basle Dragoons, 1793.
   b) Britain: Officer, Roverea's Regt, 1800.

27 a) Private, York Rangers, 1794.
   b) Musician, York Rangers, 1794.
   c) Private, Regt Royal Louis, 1794.

BRITAIN

28 a) Grenadier, Loyal Emigrants, 1796.
    b) Private, Regt Béon, 1795.
    c) Grenadier, Regt Castries, 1796.

29 a) N.C.O., Duke of Bourbon's Grenadiers,
Armée de Condé, with flag, 1799.
b) Cossack, 1799.

FRANCE

30 a) Volunteer, Army of the Rhine, 1796.
   b) Officer with Colour, 5th Demi-Brigade de Bataille, 1796.

31 a) Admiral, Royal Navy, 1794 (Lord Howe).
    b) Seaman, Royal Navy.

BRITAIN

32 a) Private, 42nd Highlanders, campaign dress, 1794.
    b) Officer, Caithness & Rothsay Fencibles, 1795.
    c) Sergeant, Sutherland Fencibles, 1795.

33 a) Trooper, St Mary (Islington) Volunteer Cavalry, 1799.
   b) Grenadier, East Yorkshire Militia, 1797.

34 a) Lady in 'uniform' of the Royal East India Company Volunteers, 1799.
    b) Private, Bridge Ward Volunteers, 1799.
    c) Private, Battalion Company, Birmingham Loyal Association, 1798.

35 a) Officer, Light Company, 12th Foot, 1796.
   b) Private, 5th Btn, 60th Foot, 1799.

AUSTRIA

36 a) Fusilier Officer, 4th Regt, 1799.
    b) Fusilier, 41st Regt, 1800.
    c) Grenadier, 33rd (Hungarian) Regt, 1800.

37 a) Officer, Light Infantry, 1800.
    b) Private, Border Infantry, 1799.
    c) Private, Lower Austrian State Corps, 1797.

38 a) France: Lancer, Polish Danube Legion, 1799–1800.
    b) Poland: 'Scytheman', Kosciusko's Army, 1794.

39 a) Batavian Republic: Grenadier, 2nd Demi-Brigade, 1797.
    b) Modena: Musician, National Guard, 1798.
    c) Modena: Grenadier, National Guard, 1798.

RUSSIA

40 a) Infantryman, campaign dress, 1799.
    b) Conscript, 1799.
    c) Infantryman, campaign dress, 1799.

41 a) France: Ensign, Navy, 1798.
    b) Ireland: Pikeman, 1798.
    c) France: Master Gunner, Navy, 1798.

FRANCE

42 a) Bonaparte, 1799.
   b) Inspecteur aux Révues, 1800.
   c) Kléber, 1798.

43 a) Grenadier, Demi-Brigades de Bataille, 1798.
    b) Fusilier, Demi-Brigades de Bataille, 1798.

FRANCE

44 a) Grenadier, 9th Demi-Brigade de Bataille, 1799.
   b) Chasseur, 21st Demi-Brigade Légère, 1800.

45 a) Grenadier Officer, 88th Demi-Brigade de Bataille, 1800.
b) Fusilier, 25th Demi-Brigade de Bataille, 1800.
c) Fusilier, 75th Demi-Brigade de Bataille, 1800.

FRANCE

46 a) Chasseur, 4th Demi-Brigade Légère, 1800.
   b) Fusilier, 88th Demi-Brigade de Bataille, 1800.
   c) Grenadier, 85th Demi-Brigade de Bataille, 1800.

47 a) Trooper, Régt des Dromadaires, 1800.
   b) Trooper, Régt des Dromadaires, 1799.

48 a) France: Mameluke, 1801.
    b) Egypt: Mameluke, 1799.

49 a) Grenadier, 61st Foot (Egypt), 1801.
   b) Private, 90th (Perthshire Volunteers) Light Infantry, 1800.

BRITAIN

50 a) Grenadier, Regt de Roll, 1798 (full dress).
   b) Officer, Regt de Roll (Egypt).
   c) Private, Regt de Roll.(Egypt).

51 a) Hanover: Officer, 4th Regt.
    b) Prussia: Officer, 5th Cuirassiers, Gala uniform.
    c) Prussia: Officer, Fusiliers of the Westphalian Brigade.

52 a) Denmark: Officer, Norwegian Guard Regt.
    b) Portugal: Officer, Olivenca Regt.

FRANCE

53 a) Trooper, 11th Chasseurs à Cheval, 1801.
    b) Trooper, 7th Hussars, 1800.

AUSTRIA

54 a) Field Marshal, 1800.
   b) Officer, Sappers, 1800.
   c) Private, Artillery, 1800.

55 a) Trooper, Dragoons, 1799.
   b) Trooper, 1st Light Dragoons, 1800.

56 a) Baden: Officer, Leib-Regt, full dress, 1802.
   b) Prussia: Officer, Magdeburg Hussars, 1800.

57 a) Naples: Private, Regt Albania, 1800.
    b) Cisalpine Republic: Fusilier Lieutenant, 1801.

FRANCE

58 a) Trooper, 8th Cavalry, campaign dress, 1800.
   b) N.C.O., 5th Dragoons, 1800.

59 a) Trooper, 1st Carabiniers, campaign dress, 1800.
    b) Driver, Artillery, 1801.

FRANCE

60 a) Trumpeter, Horse Grenadiers, Consular Guard, c.1801.
   b) Drummer, Grenadiers, Consular Guard, c.1801.

61 a) Carabinier, 14th Demi-Brigade Légère, 1800.
   b) Musician, 14th Demi-Brigade Légère, 1800.
   c) Chasseur, Light Infantry, 1801.

62 a) France: Infantryman, San Domingo, 1802.
b) France: 'Chef de Musique', San Domingo, 1802.
c) Britain: Cuban Chasseur, 1796.

63 a) Private, Battalion Company, 20th Foot, 1800–01.
    b) Officer, Light Company, 34th Foot, c.1800.

64 a) Helvetian Republic: Chasseur, Helvetian Legion, 1802.
    b) Saxony: Hussar, 1803.

Colour Plate Descriptions

FRANCE:
a) 'Sans-Culotte', 1792.
b) Private, Gardes Suisses,
1792.

The peasant/soldier of the early French republic was nicknamed 'sans-culotte', i.e. a radical so impoverished as to be 'without breeches'. The man illustrated wears typical peasant costume and a 'bonnet of liberty', the cap which became the symbol of republican France, and which was often worn by the early republican armies when there was a shortage of military head-dress. The striped trousers and bare feet or wooden clogs were likewise common during the early campaigns. Pikes (at first home-made) were supplemented by any weapons or agricultural implements which could be acquired.

The Swiss Guard was the most famous royal bodyguard in Europe, since the first employment of Swiss mercenaries by Louis IX in 1481. Their loyalty and courage was legend by the sixteenth century: 'Where', cries Claudius in *Hamlet*, 'are my Switzers? Let them guard the door.' They passed into history on 10 August 1792 at the Tuileries when, deserted by the King's republican bodyguard, they stood alone to face the Parisian mob. They repelled the crowd with ease until the King, in a misguided attempt to prevent further bloodshed, ordered them to cease fire, whereupon they were overrun and massacred, about 600 of the 900 on duty falling at their posts and a further 200 dying of wounds in prison.

Their uniform was of the distinctive red traditionally associated with Franco-Swiss corps, with dark blue facings and white lace (silver for officers). The grenadiers wore black fur caps with large brass (or silver) plate, white plume and cords and white epaulettes; drum-

mers wore 'reversed colours' (i.e. blue with red facings) and mixed red-and-white lace. Unlike the ordinary infantry, the Swiss Guard wore a waist-belt from which the sabre was suspended.

2 FRANCE:
a) Trooper,
Hussards de Chamborant,
1789–90.
b) Grenadier, 23rd Régt,
1789 (Régt du Roi).

Plates 2, 17 and 53 illustrate the evolution of French hussar dress during the Revolutionary Wars. The trooper illustrated in Plate 2, from a contemporary gouache by Lieut. Barbier of the 'Hussards de Chamborant', wears the uniform of the 'Ancien Régime', plus the new republican 'tricolor' cockade. All the classic hussar features are present: 'mirliton' cap with 'wing' which could be worn hanging loose, braided dolman and slung pelisse, with the front corners of the shabraque turned back to give easier access to the pistol-holsters, a common practice on campaign. The six hussar regiments which existed in 1789 were deprived of their 'aristocratic' titles in January 1791:

Régt de Berchény (1st Hussars, 1791): black-and-red mirliton with white cords and red-over-white plume; light blue dolman, pelisse and breeches, red cuffs, white lace and buttons.
Régt de Chamborant (2nd, 1791): sky-blue and black mirliton with white cords, red-over-white plume; brown dolman and pelisse, sky-blue breeches, white braid; Barbier shows sky-blue cuffs but Malibran gives red.
Régt d'Esterhazy (3rd, 1791): black-and-white

mirliton, red cords; grey dolman, pelisse and breeches, white buttons, red lace and cuffs.

Régt de Saxe (4th, 1791): green-and-black mirliton, white cords, green-over-white plume; green dolman and pelisse, red breeches and cuffs, yellow lace and buttons.

Régt du Colonel-Général (5th, 1791): black-and-red mirliton, yellow cords (Barbier shows red), red plume; dark blue dolman and breeches, red cuffs and pelisse, yellow lace and buttons.

Régt de Lauzun (6th, 1791): sky-blue and black mirliton, sky-blue-over-white plume, white cords (Barbier shows yellow); sky-blue dolman and breeches, white cuffs and pelisse, yellow lace and buttons.

Sabretaches had a basic design of the interlaced royal cypher, upon a cloth ground with lace edge: Berchény sky-blue with white lace (Barbier shows red/white), Chamborant red/white (Barbier red/black), Esterhazy red/white, Saxe and Colonel-Général red/yellow, Lauzun red/yellow (Barbier sky-blue/white). The sheepskin horse-furniture was edged with scalloped cloth, red for Colonel-Général and Esterhazy, sky-blue for Lauzun and Berchény (Barbier shows red for the latter), Saxe green and Chamborant brown (Barbier black). Prior to 1789 the Régt Saxe was named Conflans, and when the entire unit defected in 1792 the 5th and 6th were renumbered 4th and 5th respectively. Regulations for 1791 note that, for parade, black plumes with a tip of the regimental distinctive colour were to be worn.

The traditional hussar hairstyle consisted of a 'queue' at the rear and hanging 'cadenettes' or side-plaits from each temple. Moustaches were compulsory; when Baron de Marbot joined the 1st Hussars, too young to grow his own, he had to paint on a moustache with blacking! He records the attributes of a 'typical hussar of the old school': '... a hard drinker, a brawler, always ready for a quarrel and a fight; brave, moreover, to the point of rashness.' His own sergeant was a typical 'jolly ruffian' with 'a regular rowdy air' heightened

by an accent of 'the most barbarous French Alsatian gibberish', for the old Berchény wa largely German in composition, Germa words of command being used until 1793.

The uniform of the 23rd 'Régiment du Ro was not typical of infantry, as the unit appar ently retained an archaic style, including larg cuffs and a profusion of lace. The collar i variously depicted, that illustrated (afte Malibran) being very low and exposing th neck-band; Malibran states that the grena diers retained the old waist-belt instead of second shoulder-belt, and that the fur grena dier cap (only re-introduced in 1789) had bee worn by the 23rd throughout. When grena diers and chasseurs received red and gree epaulettes respectively in 1788, the 23r perhaps retained their old-style epaulettes.

3 FRANCE:
a) Fusilier, 42nd Line, 1791.
b) Fusilier Lieutenant, 32nd Line, 1792.

White (often with a greyish tinge) was th traditional colour of the French infantr uniform and remained as such for regula infantry until 1793–94, though, owing t shortage of material, old white uniforms wer worn until 1796–97 and Kobell shows one a late as 1799. By the 1786 regulations, regimen tal facing-colours were borne on collar, cuffs lapels and turnbacks according to Appendix (which does not include 'foreign' regiments) However, contemporary pictures suggest degree of laxity even before the Revolution cuffs including slashed varieties with flap bearing three or four buttons, or the typ without flap, with the cuff-opening edge with piping. Similarly, high and low collar are recorded, with or without piping.

The 1791 changes introduced new facing colours (see Appendix II) and a renumberin of some regiments caused, for example, by th disbanding of the 23rd in 1790. The expansio of the regular infantry in 1792 caused ye another alteration of facings for regiment which in 1791 were numbered 42 to 102 (see Appendix III), so that the regiments which in 1786 had numbered 50 to 96 had received three changes of uniform in four years. Owing to the necessity of allowing uniforms to wear out before their replacement, some of these changes can never have been implemented. The fusilier illustrated wears the shoulder-straps worn by all except grenadiers.

Infantry head-dress in 1786 consisted of the bicorn hat with white cockade (see Plate 1); grenadier caps were re-introduced in 1789. The 'tricolor' cockade was adopted in May 1790, in various designs of red, white and blue concentric circles. The crested helmet introduced in 1791 resembled the British 'Tarleton', but often appeared shoddy with imitation fur on its leather skull. Metal reinforcing-bands of various types ran up the sides of the cap. The helmet was never popular and was not received by all regiments, some apparently retaining the hat. The 46th, for example, received helmets in 1793 and wore them until 1796, by which time they were so smelly that in a mass demonstration the whole regiment threw them into the river at Strasbourg; they had to buy hats to replace them at five francs per man but seemed satisfied with the exchange. The 9th Demi-Brigade, alternatively, kept their helmets at least until 1798. White plumes with facing-coloured tip were worn in full dress; in ordinary dress they were replaced by a small pompom. The units illustrated apparently received helmets in 1791–92: the 32nd (ex-Bassigny, numbered 33 in 1786) and the 42nd (ex-Limousin, numbered 43 in 1786), both after watercolours by General Vanson. The old powdered hairstyle was retained by the ex-royal army for some time.

Equipment was standard for all companies, excepting grenadiers who wore an additional belt over the right shoulder to support their short sabre. White breeches were worn with white gaiters in summer and black in winter, officers having boots as illustrated. Epaulettes indicated their rank, the example illustrated being a lieutenant with one fringed and one unfringed shoulder-strap.

4 FRANCE:
Officer with Colour,
7th Btn, 5th Div.,
Paris National Guard
(District des Blancs-Manteaux),
1790.

The National Guard, as first formed, was composed of citizens of good character, very different from the unreliable conscripts of later years. The uniform of the provincial National Guard was standardized only in 1791, copying that of the Paris battalions, which ultimately served as a pattern for the general issue of blue uniforms for the rest of the army.

In 1789 the Paris National Guard comprised sixty 'battalions' (actually companies) arranged in six 'divisions', three or four to each of the sixteen 'quarters' of the city. The first uniform designed, with red lapels and cuffs, seems to have been little used, if at all; the later style, as illustrated, consisted of dark blue coat with red collar and white lapels, cuffs and turnbacks, and dark blue shoulder-straps piped red. The six grenadier companies wore fur caps with brass plate and white plume, and red epaulettes; the six chasseur companies had green epaulettes (some sources indicating red 'crescents') and shorter coats, dark blue or white waistcoat, red-piped dark blue breeches, red-laced dark blue girdle and short gaiters cut to resemble boots (see black-and-white Plate A). All except grenadiers wore black bicorns with 'tricolor' cockade and plumes which indicated the Division: 1st blue, 2nd red, 3rd white, 4th blue and red, 5th red, white and blue, 6th blue and white; the commander of the National Guard had a white-and-violet plume, battalion-commanders white, and aides-de-camp red; chasseurs had green or green-over-white plumes. Equipment was like that of the line infantry excepting the oval, brass cartridge-box plate bearing the Arms of Paris; musket-slings were red. Grenadiers had red grenade turnback-badges, chasseurs green hunting-horns and boats, and other red boats; the boat, a medieval cog, was the symbol of Paris.

Buttons bore the same design, plus battalion and divisional identification. One additional volunteer company, 'de la Bastille', bore a picture of the Bastille on their turnbacks and according to one source had yellow epaulettes. Officers' rank-distinctions were like those of the line plus the voluminous white sash. For the uniform of the Veteran company, see Plate 20.

The uniform authorized for the provincial National Guard in 1791 was dark blue with scarlet cuffs and collar, piped white, white lapels and cuff-flaps piped scarlet (the cuffs were often the 1786 type, without flaps). Artillery wore the same, with red turnbacks, epaulettes and plume and blue waistcoat and breeches; cavalry wore the infantry uniform with riding-boots. Prior to this, National Guard uniform (1789–91) was multi-coloured: for example the Brest corps wore scarlet, faced black, with blue-over-white plume; Avignon red faced blue and red-over-blue plume; Pont-St-Esprit white faced red and white-over-red plume; Périgueux white with blue collar, red cuffs and lapels; Chartres blue with red collar, sky-blue cuffs and lapels; Clermont blue faced carmine; Maintenon blue with red collar, yellow cuffs, lapels and shoulder-straps.

The huge Colours of the Paris battalions had many diverse designs. The one illustrated epitomizes the early spirit of the Revolution, conveyed by the motto: LIBRE SOUS UN ROI CITOYEN (an alternative version records it as LIBERTÉ SOUS UN ROI LIBRE). Presaging the national 'tricolor', it includes the Parisian ship, royal fleurs-de-lys and the letters BM, indicating the District ('de l'Église des Blancs-Manteaux') in the 'Quartier du Marais': 7th Btn, 5th Div., commanded by M. Bourdon. The Colour was presented on 12 September 1789 at a Mass of Benedictine monks; it was the gift of the ladies of the district and one source indicates a sky-blue motto-scroll and white 'cravate' (the streamer attached to the pole). See also black-and-white Plate C.

5 PRUSSIA:
a) Private,
6th Infantry Regt
(Guard Grenadiers), 1789.
b) Officer, Garde du Corps, 1790.
c) Trooper,
2nd (von Beeren) Cuirassiers, 1790.

The infantry uniform of Frederick the Great, illustrated, was worn until the somewhat half-hearted reforms of his successor Frederick William II. The 6th Regt (Guard Grenadiers) wore the tall, brass-fronted mitre cap bearing a cartouche at the bottom embossed with the royal cypher and trophies-of-arms, with the star of the Order of the Black Eagle (insignia of Guard units) and a crown above; the rear of the cap had a lower brass band embossed with bursting grenades and a red cloth upper portion with gold vertical piping. The uniform introduced for ordinary infantry by the beginning of the Revolutionary Wars (see black-and-white Plates A and B) included a blue jacket with broad lapels which could be buttoned over, red turnbacks, collar, cuffs and lapels in regimental facing-colours, and a curious hat based on the Austrian 'kaskett' with turned-up front and rear brim which could be lowered, the front bearing a metal royal cypher (for musketeers), an eagle (fusiliers) or grenade (grenadiers). An even more curious cap was issued to line grenadiers in 1799 (Guard 1798), comprising a high leather front-plate edged with black wool, with a low felt cap at the rear. In 1798 the coat became shorter and tighter and, for reasons of economy, had dummy lapels and a false waistcoat attached to the bottom of the jacket. These styles are illustrated in the Blandford Colour Series title, *Military Uniforms of the World*, Figs 154, 162 and 186. From 1794 the breeches and gaiters were protected on campaign by loose, grey canvas trousers which became white with progressive washing. 'Fusiliers' (light infantry in Prussian terminology) wore green uniforms with coloured facings.

The heavy cavalry retained the old white uniform, excepting the 2nd which had lemon-yellow. Though styled 'Cuirassiers', cuirasses had been discarded. The short-tailed coat or 'Kollet' was worn over a long waist-coat, just visible below the waist; the coat was fastened with hooks-and-eyes, with facing-colours borne on collar and cuffs, and laced on the breast, cuffs and turnbacks with regimental lace (metallic for officers); for the 2nd Cuirassiers, for example, it was red for other ranks and silver for officers, and the Garde du Corps (which ranked with the Cuirassiers despite its original 'bodyguard' status) mixed red-and-silver, and gold for officers. In place of the other ranks' coloured girdle, officers wore the silver sash with interwoven black lines common to all Prussian officers. The heavy-bladed straight sabre or 'Pallasch' often with heraldic half-basket hilt, was common to many German heavy cavalry regiments.

6 PRUSSIA:
a) **Adjutant General of Cavalry, 1790.**
b) **Trooper, 10th Hussars, 1791.**

The uniform of the Adjutant General of Cavalry (from a contemporary print) combined the features of cavalry and staff uniform, the white coat being retained (as in Plate 5). The 10th Hussars trooper is taken from a contemporary watercolour, showing typical hussar uniform, which for this unit was slightly altered in 1792 when the busby was replaced by a black 'mirliton'. Further details of Prussian hussars are given in the description of Plate 7.

7 PRUSSIA:
a) **Trooper, 9th Hussars, 1791.**
b) **N.C.O., 3rd Hussars, 1791.**

The hussar uniform which evolved from the time of Frederick the Great included laced dolman, slung pelisse (worn as a jacket in winter), white breeches (or overalls of the same colour as the pelisse), and either fur busby or 'mirliton'; few features other than equipment were standard for all regiments, though all had white plumes (black at the base for officers and at the top for N.C.O.s). Officers had silver or gold braid, silver girdles and metallic-laced belts; sabretaches were usually of the regimental colour with lace edging and an interlaced FWR cypher below a crown, though some officers' sabretaches bore heraldic devices. Trumpeters always wore mirlitons and had distinctive lace on dolman and pelisse. Horse-furniture was of the standard pattern illustrated, the shabraque regimentally-coloured and the cylindrical valise usually of the shabraque-colour with coloured piping around the circular ends. Regimental details were as follows.

1st Regt: Brown busby, dark green bag, white cords; light green dolman, dark green pelisse with white fur and braid; red girdle with white barrels; dark green shabraque with light green vandyke design edged white, dark green valise edged light green; light green sabretache with white lace. From 1798 all light green was changed to dark green.

2nd Regt: Brown busby, red bag, white cords; scarlet dolman with dark blue collar and cuffs, white braid; dark blue pelisse with white fur and braid; dark blue girdle with white barrels; dark blue shabraque with scarlet vandyke edged white, dark blue valise edged scarlet; red sabretache with white lace. Officers had gold lace, and for parade wore yellow boots, a tiger-skin cloak and an eagle's wing on the busby. The harness of all ranks was covered with cowrie-shells; white-laced dark blue breeches were also worn.

3rd Regt: Brown busby, white bag, red cords; white dolman with yellow cuffs, collar and braid; dark blue pelisse with white fur and yellow braid; yellow girdle with white barrels; yellow sabretache with white lace. Dark blue shabraque with white vandyke edged yellow, dark blue valise edged yellow. Dolman changed to dark blue in 1800.

4th Regt: Brown busby, sky-blue bag, white cords; sky-blue dolman and pelisse with mixed white-and-sky-blue braid, white pelisse-fur; yellow girdle with white barrels; white sabretache with sky-blue lace; sky-blue shabraque and valise with mixed white-and-sky-blue braid.

5th Regt: Black mirliton bearing a white metal skull over crossed bones and black 'wing'; black dolman with red collar and cuffs; black pelisse with black fur (white for officers); white braid; red girdle with white barrels. Black shabraque with red vandyke edged white, black valise edged red. Plain black sabretaches, officers' red with silver lace, bearing a black eagle on a silver disc in the centre.

6th Regt: Black mirliton with white cords; greyish-brown dolman with yellow collar and cuffs; greyish-brown pelisse with white fur; yellow braid; yellow girdle with white barrels; greyish-brown sabretache with yellow lace; greyish-brown shabraque with yellow vandyke, greyish-brown valise edged yellow.

7th Regt: Black mirliton with black wing edged white, white cords; officers' wings silver. Yellow dolman with sky-blue collar and cuffs; sky-blue pelisse with black fur; white braid; sky-blue girdle with white barrels; sky-blue sabretache with white lace; sky-blue shabraque with yellow vandyke and white edging.

8th Regt: Black mirliton; dark red dolman with black collar and cuffs; dark red pelisse with black fur; white braid; dark red shabraque with black vandyke and white edging.

9th Regt: Recruited from Bosnians and wearing an individual uniform, only the shabraque being like that of other regiments. Astrakhan cap, short jacket without braid as shown; 'lancer'-style girdle. Alternatively, a dark blue knee-length frock-coat with white fur collar and cuffs, with white braid down the front and around the skirts as on the short jacket. Officers wore brown busbies with red cloth top but without a bag, scarlet frock-coats with dark blue collar and cuffs and pelisse-style braiding in summer, and dark blue frocks

with red facings in winter; silver lace. Officers' shabraques had dark blue vandykes. N.C.O.s had three loops of white braid on the breast, and lance-pennons bearing an eagle and an embroidered sun. In 1799 all Prussians were transferred from the unit, it being then formed as a corps of Polish 'Towarczys' (noblemen), in which the front rank of each squadron was composed of lesser nobility and the middle and rear ranks of troopers. The 9th was the only regiment armed with lances.

10th Regt: Brown busby, yellow bag piped red, red-and-white cords; yellow dolman with dark blue collar and cuffs; dark blue pelisse with white fur; red braid (silver for officers); dark blue shabraque with yellow vandyke edged red; dark blue valise edged red; red girdle with dark blue barrels. Black mirlitons replaced the busby in 1792; from 1801 dark blue dolman faced straw-yellow and dark blue breeches were worn.

In general, N.C.O.s' pelisse-fur was a contrasting colour to that of the men (usually fawn, sometimes black as for the 6th); sword-and pouch-belts for all other ranks were brown leather (9th black); only the carbine-belt, not worn by officers and N.C.O.s, was white.

8 BRITAIN:
**a) Sergeant,
Battalion Company,
2nd Foot Guards, 1792.
b) Officer,
Battalion Company,
2nd Foot Guards, 1792.
c) Grenadier,
2nd Foot Guards, 1792.**

Plates 8 and 9 illustrate British infantry uniform of the early 1790s, the Foot Guards' version from watercolours by Edward Dayes. The bicorn hat, usually worn with one corner angled over the right eye, was usually unlaced but with a small feather (worsted tuft for other ranks) and the national black cockade. The ed coat (scarlet for officers and senior N.C.O.s) had collar (usually of the 'standing' variety, replacing the old 'stand-and-fall' type), cuffs and lapels (and shoulder-straps for other ranks) of the facing-colour, with varied arrangements of lace loops on lapels and cuffs; officers had metallic lace and sergeants white (metallic for some regiments, for example gold for the Guards), and lower ranks white lace with interwoven coloured lines in regimental pattern. Distinctive to the Guards was lace edging to collar and cuffs. Lace loops were spaced evenly or in pairs (in threes for the 3rd Foot Guards), either square-ended, pointed (as illustrated), or in the wider-pointed 'bastion' shape. The white turnbacks were usually fastened by a regimental button and strip of lace; Guards' turnbacks were edged with red-edged white lace. Waistcoat and breeches were white. Officers' distinctions included lace epaulettes, crimson waist-sash and (when on duty) gilt gorget with facing-coloured rosettes and ribbons. Equipment consisted of white leather shoulder-belts supporting cartridge-box and bayonet, and a knapsack usually painted in the facing-colour, bearing a device such as the 2nd Guards' Star of the Order of the Garter, or a legend, such as GUARDS/THIRD REGIMENT. Shoulder-belts were secured by an oval metal 'breastplate', usually brass, officers' plates being finely wrought in gilt, silver and enamel. Those illustrated, for example, bore an engraved Garter Star, the officers having an enamelled silver star. Sergeants were identified by fringed shoulder-straps, waist-sash (ultimately crimson with a facing-coloured central stripe) and halberd, which from 1792 was supplanted by the half-pike or 'spontoon'.

Flank companies—grenadiers and light infantry—wore distinctive items of uniform, such as the white-plumed grenadier cap, the pattern of which varied: the 1st Guards, for example, had a cap with black-enamelled plate bearing the Royal Arms in silver (gilt for sergeants) and red-tipped plume, the 2nd Guards a small Royal Arms badge (gilt for sergeants), and the 3rd an old-style pointed cap with white metal plate (gilt for sergeants).

Regimental light companies usually wore shorter jackets and a leather cap or 'round hat' (see Plate 35). All flank companies usually had 'wings' on the shoulders, red cloth for the line and dark blue for Guards, with lace trimming. Note the ornamental match-case on the grenadier's belt, a relic of the use of hand-grenades in combat.

Details of regimental uniform can often only be gleaned from contemporary pictures or the annual 'Inspection Returns'. For example, the random details for line regiments for 1789–92 below are taken from Dayes' pictures and various Returns.

1st Foot: Blue facings; lace in pairs: officers' gold, O.R.s' with blue 'cable'. White plumes, black-tipped for officers. Officers' hats gold-laced.

2nd Foot: Blue facings; lace in pairs: officers' silver, O.R.s with blue stripe. White hat-lace (officers' silver); white plume with blue tip for O.R.s; black for officers.

3rd Foot: Buff facings; lace in pairs, with yellow, red and black stripes (officers' silver); hats much smaller than regulation, edged white (officers' silver); black plumes.

4th Foot: Blue facings; lace in pairs, with blue 'worm' (officers' silver); white hat-lace (officers' silver); no plume.

5th Foot: Dull green facings; lace evenly-spaced, with two red stripes (officers' silver); white hat-lace (officers' silver), white plumes.

6th Foot: 'Philamot yellow' facings (origin: 'feuille mort' = dead-leaf colour); lace in pairs, with red and yellow stripe (officers' silver); no plume or hat-lace.

7th Foot: Blue facings; lace in pairs, with blue stripe (officers' gold); fur cap with white plume, gold cords for officers.

8th Foot: Blue facings; lace evenly-spaced, with blue and yellow stripes (officers' gold); white hat-lace (officers' gold); no plume according to Dayes but 1788 Returns note: 'black tufts to the hats.'

9th Foot: Yellow facings; lace with black stripe (officers' silver); white hat-lace (officers' silver), white plumes.

15th Foot: Yellow facings; lace with one red

and one mixed black-and-yellow stripe; officers' hat-lace silver; white plumes.

17th Foot: Hats noted (1791): '... smaller than the ... regulation.'

21st Foot: 1791 Returns note: 'Officers clothed and armed as Fuzileers', i.e. with fur cap and carbines; 'Non. Coms. armed with carbines'.

22nd Foot: 1788 Returns note white feathers and 'linen trousers and white gaiters'.

23rd Foot: 1788 Returns note three feathers worn on hats, imitating Prince of Wales' crest.

29th Foot: Yellow facings; lace in pairs, with two yellow stripes edged black (officers' silver); white hat-lace (officers' silver), other ranks only with yellow-tipped white plume. 1789 Returns note: 'Officers ... have adopted the use of feathers'; and 1791: 'Clothing very short in waist, and the lapels are not to the full length of the bottom of it. ... Hats ... so small as to make it necessary to tie them on. Regiment wears worsted tufts in imitation of feathers.'

30th Foot: 1791 Returns note: 'Battalion furnished with feathers at 1s. each.'

31st Foot: 1791 Returns note: 'Hats too small in the crown ... Light Infantry are so small as not to go on the head, but are tied on.'

33rd Foot: 1791 Returns note: 'Officers' hair without curl and hanging loose'; same remark about smallness of hats.

34th Foot: 1791 Returns note: hats too small, bound with narrower lace than usual; 'Men have feathers at 7d. each.'

9 BRITAIN:
a) **Officer, 1st Foot, 1794.**
b) **Private, Grenadier Company, 36th Foot, 1791.**
c) **Sergeant, Grenadier Company, 36th Foot, 1791.**

The officer illustrated is taken from a portrait of John Clayton Cowell of the 1st Foot (Royal Scots), by Sir William Beechey, c. 1794–95 Of especial note are the soft leather boot which could be pushed down around the ankle, a style often reserved for undres uniform.

The grenadiers wear a particularly splendi version of 'flank company' dress, from Rober Home's picture of the siege of Bangalor (1791). The hats have an unusually larg plume and (apparently) a single huge tassel with an ornate fringe-and-lace design on th cockade. The coat has the old-style 'turn down' collar with a lace loop on each side standing collars had been seen as early as 178 (Inspection Return, 2nd Foot) but the ol type lasted for some years. The flank company wings have straps not of the facing colour but either white with red edges o covered in regimental lace. Design o sergeants' lace is not clear from the picture either white or possibly silver; the sash i crimson mixed with the facing-colour Further company distinctions were th grenade-shaped cartridge-box plate bearin GR on the ball, and the small belt-plate bearin the same device. The elaborately-braide hair-style (apparently lightly-powdered i some cases) was complemented by the wearin of moustaches, an unorthodox feature bu apparently compulsory for this company, a General Meadows addressed them at Bangal ore by the term 'moustaches'. The regimenta light company wore tail-less jackets witl wings, and fur-crested, peaked leather hel mets.

The grenadiers wear one-piece 'gaiter trousers' as a concession to tropical dress, bu otherwise have European uniform. It wa usual, however, for units in the tropics (par ticularly West Indies) to wear short re jackets, trousers, and some type of 'roune hat'; for example, the 14th Foot's 179 Inspection Return: '... disembarked ... from Jamaica ... linen waistcoats and long trouser-breeches of the West Indies ...', anc the 15th Foot, also 1791 (Orders): 'Hats ... shall be made round, and bordered with a narrow lace ... much more proper for a warm climate. ...'.

10 HANOVER:
    a) **Officer, 3rd Cavalry, 1790.**
    b) **Private,**
    14th Light Infantry, 1794.

King George III of England being Elector of Hanover, the Hanoverian army's uniforms were strongly influenced by those of Britain. Certain features were common for all arms: officers' yellow sashes and white-over-yellow plumes and other ranks' yellow-over-white plumes. The officer is taken from a watercolour by H. B. Merker, a Hanoverian artillery subaltern. All the cavalry wore blue with coloured facings: 1st (Leib) Regt red; 2nd Cavalry, 4th, 5th and 8th Dragoons white; 3rd Cavalry, 6th and 7th Dragoons yellow; gold lace for the 1st, 2nd and 9th and silver for the remainder (yellow and white respectively for other ranks). Only the Leib-Garde (equivalent to the British Life Guards) had scarlet coats, with dark blue lapels, gold lace (including loops on collar and cuffs) and gold-laced hats. The two light dragoon regiments wore blue with scarlet facings and laced lapels, with three chevrons on the lower sleeve, lace gold for the 9th (Queen's) Light Dragoons and silver for the 10th (Prince of Wales'). Both wore the leather helmet which is being examined by the officer illustrated: black with a crest edged with scalloped metal, an asymmetrical front-plate edged with metal and bearing the Hanoverian white horse, and a falling horsehair mane.

Infantry uniforms also copied British patterns, including bicorn hat and red coat. Regimental details according to Merker: facing-colours dark green for 1st, 6th, 7th and 10th Regts; 2nd dark blue; 3rd and 11th black; 4th and 13th slate-blue; 5th and 12th yellow; 8th and 9th white. Officers' lace silver; other ranks' shoulder-straps facing-coloured for 1st, 4th, 9th and 12th; scarlet for 2nd, 5th, 6th, 8th, 10th, 11th and 13th; 3rd and 7th white. Landwehr (militia) had white facings and Garrison Battns red. Regimental grenadiers had fur caps; Foot Guards had infantry uniform with blue facings and gold lace. Cocked hats were edged with white lace,

though wide-brimmed 'round hats' with one brim turned up are shown worn by the composite 1st Grenadier Btn in the 1793 campaign, with white feather and edging (yellow-and-white feathers for officers). Equipment was like that of the British, though one source shows red musket-slings. The closed jacket and 'stovepipe' shako were introduced about the same time as in the British army.

The old 14th and 15th Regts were transferred to East India Company service in 1787, and a new 14th Light Infantry raised in 1793; the uniform comprised 'round hat', grey jacket faced green, buff leather breeches and black equipment; officers had gold lace and the usual yellow sash but no gorget. Jäger companies had green jackets and waistcoats, yellowish leather breeches, grey gaiters and yellow lace and epaulettes (officers' gold).

11 HANOVER:
    a) **Pontooneer, 1790.**
    b) **Sapper, 1790.**
    c) **Driver, Train, 1790.**

Merker's paintings include a selection of uniforms of the 'supporting services'—engineers and supply-corps. The Engineer corps (Pontooneers, Pioneers and Sappers & Miners) wore blue uniform with red facings and dark blue collar with red patch, the main distinction between branches being the headgear. Pontooneers and Pioneers wore black 'round hats' with yellow band and edging, with a turned-up rear brim bearing either crossed anchors or crossed axe, pick and spade respectively; feathers were either black or mixed black, red and yellow. The Sappers & Miners wore small black leather caps (or possibly a light dragoon-style helmet with red horsehair mane) bearing a crown-over-GR badge on the front, and on the rear flap a badge of crossed swords and gabion (Sappers) or crossed picks and flaming powder-barrel (Miners). The GR badge may have been worn on the front of the 'round hats' as well. All carried sabres with lion-head pommel. Officers had gold lace and gold-laced bicorn hats.

Drivers of the Artillery Train wore the uniform illustrated, with dark blue brassard bearing a yellow GR; a long, single-breasted red greatcoat with shoulder-length cape was also worn. At a later date a low, round peaked cap of green cloth with a red crown was apparently worn, with a blue brassard on each arm bearing a red GR. Merker shows staff of the Military Train wearing cavalry uniform (the coat minus lapels) consisting of bicorn, blue coat with red collar, red turnbacks for an officer and blue for an N.C.O., the officer with a gold aiguillette and the N.C.O.s mixed gold-and-red. Artificers attached to the Train wore a uniform like Artillery Train drivers, but of blue with collar denoting the trade: wheelwright buff, smith black, saddler blue, etc.

The Artillery wore infantry-style uniform of bicorn, light blue coat faced red, gold officers' lace and epaulettes, light blue shoulder-straps for other ranks, and legwear like the infantry.

12 BADEN/SAXONY:
a) BADEN: Trooper,
Garde du Corps, 1790.
b) SAXONY: Trooper,
Kurfürst Cuirassiers, 1785.

Plate 12 illustrates two versions of Germanic heavy cavalry uniform, with the traditional white or straw-yellow coat. The Baden Garde du Corps (the Margrave of Baden's body-guard) comprised three companies, one dressed as dragoons, one cuirassiers, and the guard company illustrated wearing the livery of the house of Baden (yellow and red), with red-and-white lace on both uniform and belts. Officers had a 'gala' dress consisting of a hat similar to that illustrated, with silver scalloped-lace edge, scarlet coat without lapels, cut open to expose the waistcoat, with yellow collar, cuffs and turnbacks, and eight silver figure-of-eight loops with a tassel at the end on each side of the breast, one loop on each side of the collar and two above each cuff. Yellow waistcoat; silver-and-red waist-sash

worn over the waistcoat but below the coat, and legwear as illustrated.

The Saxon cuirassier wears a uniform basically unchanged until 1810, the hat becoming progressively larger and a white plume being added in 1794. The typical German cuirass consisted of a black-enamelled front-plate held with cross-straps at the rear, minus back-plate; this unprotected rear proved a great disadvantage when cuirassiers so clad engaged in a mêlée with cuirassiers wearing complete protection.

13 BAVARIA:
a) Fusilier,
11th Regt 'Preysing', 1790.
b) Fusilier Corporal,
5th Regt 'Wahl', 1790.

Plate 13 illustrates the uniform introduced in 1784–88 during the 'reforms' of Graf von Rumford (Benjamin Thompson, an American who became Bavarian War Minister). For all except officers in undress and court dress, the bicorn was replaced by the 'Rumford Kaskett', a crested leather helmet with large brass plate bearing the Bavarian royal arms and a lion-head at the front of the crest, and a falling horsehair mane, white for staff, grenadiers and cavalry and black for all others; the helmet was in common use by 1788. From 1784 the infantry wore a white coat with half-lapels, opening to expose a 'waistcoat' which, due to Rumford's stringent economy, was actually a dummy front sewn on to the coat. Collar, cuffs, lapels and turnbacks were facing-coloured, the collar having a linen band sewn into it to resemble the upper edge of a stock, a further economy measure, as were the one-piece gaiter-trousers made to resemble breeches and boots. Initially facing-coloured shoulder-straps were worn, but from 1790 black leather epaulettes with brass crescent and chain-edging, worn on both the jacket and the calf-length, ash-grey greatcoat. Rank-distinction was in the number of buttons on the half-lapels: 2nd Lieut. and Major three, Lieut. and Lieut. Colonel four, Captain and

Colonel five, the higher ranks in each case having metallic lace loops of the button-colour. All other ranks had five buttons, with tape of the button-colour on the top hole for lance-corporals, the top two for corporals, sergeants three, quartermaster-sergeant four and sergeant-major five.

Facing-colours were cornflower-blue for the 1st and 2nd Grenadiers, 3rd and 4th Grenadiers dark blue, 1st and 2nd Regts red, 3rd and 4th Regts brick-red, 5th and 6th yellow, 7th and 8th green, 9th and 10th peach-pink, 11th and 12th crimson, 13th and 14th black. The first of each pair listed above had white metal buttons and the remainder brass. The two Jäger regiments had light green uniforms (including waistcoat and breeches), black facings and equipment, white metal buttons for the 1st and brass for the 2nd.

The 'economy' uniforms were a total failure: in wet weather the helmet-manes clung to the neck and made the men 'look like savages', as General Wrede said; after fording a river the false gaiters could not be removed but had to dry on the legs, and the false-fronted coats were no protection against the cold. From 1798 to 1800 Maximilian Joseph IV of Bavaria redesigned the uniform completely, returning to the hitherto traditional cornflower-blue uniform with wool-crested 'raupenhelm'; see *Uniforms of the Retreat from Moscow*, Plate 35.

14 BAVARIA:
a) **Trooper,**
Chevauleger
Regt Fugger,
1792.
b) **Trooper,**
Minucci Cuirassiers, 1792.

Plate 14 illustrates the cavalry version of the 'Rumford' uniform: the same helmet as in Plate 13 but with a white mane. The three types of cavalry (cuirassiers, dragoons and chevaulegers) were distinguished only by their uniform, the cuirass having been abandoned

in 1785. The coat was white for the two cuirassier and two dragoon regiments, and light green for the three chevauleger corps. Both cuirassier regiments (1st Minucci and 2nd Winkelhausen) had scarlet lapels and cuffs and either scarlet or white edged scarlet turn-backs; their waistcoats were white and breeches 'yellow' (buff-leather). The 1st and 2nd Dragoons had black facings as above, and similar waistcoat and breeches; the 1st and 2nd Chevaulegers had black facings, the 3rd apple-green, and green waistcoats. In all cases the collars were of the coat-colour. Buttons were brass for the 2nd Cuirassiers, 2nd Dragoons and 2nd Chevaulegers and white metal for the remainder.

The heavy regiments carried straight-bladed 'Pallasch'-type sabres worn from a shoulder-belt; the chevaulegers had curved sabres with half-basket hilts. The chevaulegers' horse-furniture was as illustrated; the heavy cavalry had cloth shabraques with holster-caps, for example the Minucci Regt's shabraque and holster-caps were scarlet with a broad edging of white and sky-blue chequerboard lace. The overalls worn by the chevauleger illustrated were used on active service instead of the 'yellow' breeches and top-boots. Although hair was still powdered and worn in a 'queue' with a roll over each ear, the light cavalry were allowed to wear moustaches of their own hair-colour, no longer being compelled to blacken their moustaches to provide a uniform appearance!

15 AUSTRIA:
a) **Fusilier, 42nd Regt,**
1792.
b) **Dragoon,**
campaign dress, 1789.
c) **Officer,**
Wurmser's Friekorps, 1793.

Contrasting with the Austrian uniforms of other plates, three campaign uniforms are illustrated in Plate 15. The simple infantry uniform became the pattern for the more functional uniforms adopted by many armies.

From 1769–70 all infantry (except grenadiers who retained their fur caps) wore the 'Kaskett', a small leather cap with raised front and without peak, bearing a large national pompom-cockade on the left and large brass plate on the front, embossed with the Imperial cypher until 1790 when the Imperial double-eagle was substituted. This cap (worn until the adoption of the 'classical' helmet in 1798) was the forerunner of the peaked shako; though the false-fronted British 'Belgic' shako of 1812 probably owed its design to the Portuguese 'barretina' cap, the resemblance to the 'Kaskett' is obvious. The Austrian infantry jacket was closed to the waist and had the facing-colour borne on collar, cuffs, shoulder-straps and in some cases probably on a line of piping down the breast; there was no lace whatever on the jacket, even officers having no epaulettes. They were distinguished by the national gold-and-black sash and bicorn hat, though on active service usually wore the 'Kaskett' so as not to present an obvious target to sharpshooters. The infantry equipment included the knapsack slung over the shoulder (not yet worn on the back), with a wide-bladed sabre worn not only by grenadiers but also fusiliers until 1798. The manner of wearing the waist-belt (which supported the sabre and bayonet) is variously shown, both over and under the jacket, which is sometimes depicted greater than waist-length. Though the uniform was officially superseded in 1798, contemporary artists show the 'Kaskett' and shoulder-knapsack in use as late as 1799–1800.

The single-breasted coat was also worn by the Austrian cavalry, with the bicorn hat until the 1798 helmet was introduced; but during the Austro-Turkish War (1788–89) the archaic dress illustrated (from extant items) was worn, including black-enamelled cuirass and 'lobster-tail' helmet which was apparently known as a 'Pickelhaube', not of course the famous nineteenth-century version. The whole ensemble more resembled a trooper of the Thirty Years War than a 'modern' Austrian dragoon.

The third figure's dress is even more bizarre, an unofficial 'campaign dress' of Wurmser's Styrian Friekorps, a unit raised in Slavonia in 1793 and engaged in Alsace. Drawn from life by Mechel, only the tall 'Kaskett', Austrian cockade and traditional oak-sprig proclaim his nationality; although blue with red facings was the established colouring of the unit, the appearance, including Caucasian sabre and pistols thrust in the belt, more closely resembles the dress of a Balkan bandit.

16 FRANCE:
Infantry privates, 1793.

French infantry uniform was officially changed in 1793 from white to the blue of the National Guard, though white remained in use for some time, generally conforming to the pattern illustrated. Officially the blue uniform had red collar and cuffs piped white, white lapels, turnbacks and cuff-flaps piped red; but in practice it was common to see the old-style flapless cuff, blue cuff-flaps with white or red piping, or even red cuff-flaps and lapels. The authorized shoulder-straps were blue with red piping, but it appears that the grenadiers' traditional red epaulettes were worn indiscriminately, as was the drooping red horsehair plume. The white waistcoat often had red collar and cuffs, and legwear consisted of white breeches and white or black gaiters. Due to chronic shortages, many items of civilian clothing were pressed into service, one of the figures illustrated having a striped waistcoat and both wearing the ticken trousers which became the hallmark of the early republican armies. Gaiters were frequently not worn, or worn over bare feet; wooden clogs (often stuffed with straw) were very common, whilst many units were completely barefoot. The regulation cocked hat had black tape edging and a 'tricolor' cockade held by a yellow lace loop, behind which it was usual to stick a pipe or spoon; one figure, however, has a smaller, neater hat, dating from the 'Ancien Régime', all manner of outdated stocks being utilized. Equipment was also rudimentary, canvas haversacks often replacing the knapsack. Sabres (a traditional grenadier distinction) were carried indiscriminately, and shortages of bayonet-scabbards meant that some were permanently 'fixed'. If the costume of 'les bleus' often befitted a dirty scarecrow, their weapons were often little better; one man illustrated carries the regulation 1777-pattern musket, but the other has a 1763 musketoon. So serious was the shortage of firearms that not only were outdated weapons used, but a gun called a 'fusil dépareillé' was common, a hybrid musket cobbled together from scrap and spare parts of many ancient patterns.

17 FRANCE:
a) Trooper,
Hussards de la Morte,
full dress, 1793.
b) Officer,
Hussards de la Liberté,
1792.
c) Trooper, 4th Hussars,
campaign dress, 1799.

Plate 17 continues the development of French hussar uniform from Plate 2. In November 1792 two volunteer corps (Boyer's and Lamothe's) became the 7th and 8th Hussars; the emigration of the 4th in 1793 caused the renumbering of Regts 5 to 8 as 4 to 7. In the same year the 8th, 9th and 10th Hussars were formed from the Fabrefonds volunteers, the 2nd 'Hussards de la Liberté' and the 'Hussards noirs du Nord', and the 11th newly-created; in 1794 the 12th and in 1795 the 13th were added, the original 'Hussards de la Liberté' having been given in 1792 the unusual number '7 bis', meaning (approximately) 7½ or '7 again'! Regular hussar uniform changed little, though sometimes the braiding was simplified and non-essential buttons removed as an economy measure; colouring is listed in Appendix IV, some details conflicting, probably due to shortages of material. For example, the 6th is shown with blue pelisse and the 12th with brown pelisse, dolman and breeches with white

collar, cuffs, braid and pelisse-fur. The 'surtout' coat was also worn, a functional garment usually the colour of the dolman, though the 7th had blue and the 9th and 12th sky-blue, and the 13th had scarlet cuffs. Sashes were crimson with barrels of the lace-colour, except the 3rd which had white barrels. The mirliton was worn with the wing wrapped around the body of the cap, as worn by the 4th Hussars illustrated (after Kobell). Plume-colours varied, usually black with red tip (grey tip for the 11th), except the 10th and 12th which had drooping red plumes, though variations are recorded. During this period detachable peaks were sometimes worn, adumbrating the shako of Plate 53; overalls came into use for active service. Sabretache-design varied, often comprising republican symbols (lictor's fasces, Phrygian cap) with or without a large regimental number, often on a red background. Both Kobell and Seele show the unusual pattern illustrated, with rounded bottom edge. The sheepskin shabraques had scalloped cloth edging as listed in Appendix IV.

Among the volunteer corps raised at the beginning of the Revolutionary Wars were the 'Death Hussars', named from their sombre uniform. The first unit was raised by Citizen Mairiaux in November 1792 with the title 'Hussards de Jemappes' or 'Hussards noirs du Nord'; they wore black dolman, pelisse, breeches, waistcoat and 'surtout', scarlet cuffs, white pelisse-fur, lace and buttons, black mirliton with black wing edged white and drooping red plume, black overalls and red sabretache-face and shabraque-edging. In 1793 General Dumourier organized several similar companies, usually styled 'Hussards de la Morte', wearing similar dress but with mixed black-and-white braid, white skull-and-crossed-bones on the upper sleeves of dolman and pelisse, black cuffs, red waistcoat, white sash with black barrels, black sabretache with white edging, bearing the skull and crossed bones and motto: LA RÉPUBLIQUE UNE ET INDIVISABLE OU LA MORT; black-over-white plume, white sheepskin with black edging.

The 'Hussards de la Liberté' (later '7 bis') were another volunteer unit, of which two corps were raised in 1792, at Paris and Lille. Probably only the officers wore the fur cap, though it may have been used by other ranks as well. The officer illustrated wears the ordinary 'habit' coat, with waistcoat underneath, but with the addition of hussar braiding; that it was actually worn is confirmed by a suggestion of commander, Col. Westermann, that for reasons of economy the coat- and waistcoat-braid should be discontinued (26 June 1793). For other ranks the braid was white; the rank of 'Sous-Lieutenant' is indicated by the single band of silver lace on thigh and cuff. The regiment attempted to have the ridiculous '7 bis' number replaced, hoping to be accepted as the 7th Hussars proper, but eventually were converted to the 28th Dragoons.

Other volunteer hussar units included the 'Hussards de l'Égalité' (white pelisse with grey fur, scarlet dolman, blue breeches, yellow lace, mirliton with red wing edged yellow), 'Hussards de la Montagne' (brown dolman and pelisse, sky-blue breeches, yellow lace, mirliton with sky-blue wing edged black, black plume), and 'Hussards des Alpes' (sky-blue dolman and breeches, scarlet collar, cuffs and pelisse, yellow lace, mirliton with scarlet wing edged black, white plume with red tip).

18 FRANCE:
  a) **Private,**
  Volontaires de Santerre.
  b) **Officer,**
  Vendéan rebels
  (Marquis de Lescure).
  c) **Vendéan infantryman.**

The 'uniform' of the Royalist counter-revolutionaries in the Vendée was almost exclusively civilian dress with the addition of certain distinctive marks. All members of the 'Grande Armée Catholique et Royale' wore the 'Sacré-coeur' badge, a brown cloth backing-patch sewn or pinned on the jacket, upon which was sewn or embroidered the sacred heart of Christ surmounted by a red cross, usually on a white ground. Other common features included the kerchief worn on the head, under the hat, and the use by officers of white sashes, brassards and handkerchiefs, the latter used for signalling. Being a largely peasant army, wooden 'sabots' were more common than boots. Similarly, weapons (until some were captured from the republicans) consisted of agricultural tools, crude pikes and clubs; many Vendéans carried cow-horns, the mournful bellowing of which invariably struck fear into the republicans.

Several descriptions of the costume of Vendéan leaders are recorded; the Marquis de Lescure is shown in typical civilian dress of the minor gentry, with sacré-coeur insignia, white sash and brassard and Royalist hat-cockade. He never carried a weapon: 'In a war in which generals were constantly engaged in hand to hand fighting, M. Lescure never personally killed a single man', his wife wrote. Instead, he carried '. . . an ancient sword, dating from the time of Charlemagne, dangling from his wrist, but this was merely an insignia; his only weapon was a whip . . .'. Another 'general', Nicholas Stofflet, always wore a white kerchief on his head, 'rendering him conspicuous from afar'; and Charette always wore a white head-scarf with red spots, underneath a high-crowned 'round hat' with narrow brim turned up at the front, with two gold bands around, initially with a white plume and later three—the white Bourbon colour, black for mourning and green for hope. His civilian riding-coat was either hunting-green, blue, or 'snuff'-coloured, with buckskin breeches and brown-topped riding-boots, with the usual white sash. A few ex-regulars joined the insurgents, wearing their old Royalist uniforms, including some Swiss Guard and particularly grenadiers from the Régt de Provence (4th Line), their sky-blue-faced white uniforms worn inside-out revealing the lining, with white paper hat-cockades. At the end of the rebellion the entire 'army' was in rags—for example, one young Vendéan was killed wearing nothing but two ragged skirts, one around the waist and another around the neck. Similar costumes were worn by the 'Chouans', counterrevolutionaries taking their name from their leader, Jean Cottereau, 'chouan' being a local name for the 'chouette' or screech-owl, whose call was imitated by the Breton insurgents as a battle-cry.

The 'Volontaires de Santerre', raised in 1792 to fight the Vendéan rebels, wore infantry uniform of distinctive colouring and including the double-breasted Breton waistcoat. In common with other republican forces, the majority employed against the Royalists were dressed in ragbag clothing, especially Kléber's Army of Mayence: 'I have never seen anything so filthy as these sons of liberty', wrote the Comte de Deux-Ponts, whilst Goethe described them as dressed for a harlequinade: 'One might have thought that King Edwin had opened his magic mountain and let loose his joyous army of trolls.' A few units raised for service against the Royalists wore more flamboyant costume, such as the dragoon squadron formed at Nantes from freed Negro slaves: the so-called 'American Legion', dressed in yellow coats and sky-blue breeches.

19 FRANCE:
  a) Officer, Artillery,
  1792.
  b) Private,
  Légion des Allobroges,
  1792.

The officer (from a contemporary painting) wears artillery uniform, the 1786 regulations prescribing a blue coat with scarlet cuffs; variations were recorded as in this case, the cuffs being blue and the collar scarlet. Other ranks wore blue shoulder-straps piped red. Blue lapels and breeches were worn by all artillery, excepting 'ouvriers' (unskilled personnel) who had scarlet lapels and waistcoats. The officer illustrated has a 'tricolor' cockade and carries a workmanlike sabre with 'tricolor' knot and, at the intersection of blade and hilt, a woollen pompom intended to pre-

vent the sword becoming jammed in the scabbard. Until 1792 the artillery wore buttons inscribed 64, the artillery (somewhat illogically) ranking as the 64th regiment of the line.

The term 'legion' implied a self-contained miniature army within the one unit: infantry, cavalry, transport and often artillery. The Légion des Allobroges was formed in 1792, comprising fourteen companies of light infantry, three of dragoons and one of artillery. Light infantry uniform was worn, with furcrested helmet; the cavalry had similar uniform and helmet plus hussar-boots with red lace and tassels. Their white sheepskin shabraques had red 'wolf-tooth' edging. There was no 'facing' colour, collar, lapels and cuffs being the colour of the body of the garment, though possibly turnbacks were red. The artillery wore infantry uniform with white belts instead of the black worn by other companies. In 1793 the unit was broken up, personnel passing to infantry and cavalry units.

20 FRANCE:
  a) Veteran,
  Paris National Guard, 1790.
  b) Student, École de Mars,
  1794.
  c) Lady 'pikeman', 1794.

The Paris National Guard (see Plate 4) had a Veteran company, wearing ordinary uniform with white epaulettes, sash, 'round hat' with feather panache and 'tricolor' band, the white part lettered LA NATION, LA LOI, LE ROI. The version illustrated (after Hoffman) shows the veteran armed with half-pike; other sources indicate that a sabre and brace of pistols were also carried. In 1790 the uniform of provincial National Guard veterans was modified by the adoption of a single-breasted coat without lapels, with red collar, cuffs, turnbacks, epaulettes and piping, and the sash transferred to the waist, with arms a pike and sabre. This uniform was introduced about the middle of 1791, and in 1794 a blue coat with blue collar and cuffs and red lapels, piped white on the collar and cuffs and scarlet elsewhere.

The Military Academy, established in 1794, had the romantic title 'École de Mars' and an equally romantic uniform designed by the artist Jacques-Louis David. The resulting ensemble comprised a 'Polish tunic' and ornate cap, open-necked shirt and long red scarf, tight breeches, white leather shoulder-piece with scalloped edging, waist-belt-cum-cartridge-box covered in imitation, painted leopardskin, a sword-belt emblazoned ÉGALITÉ and LIBERTÉ, and a 'glaive' in supposed imitation of the ancient Roman 'gladius'. Infantry companies wore half-gaiters, cavalry hussar boots with red lace edging and tassel and light cavalry sabres. Colouring of tunic and breeches seems to have been arbitrary, blue and red respectively with gold braid being one variation. The whole uniform, the epitome of the romantic movement in art, was probably the most bizarre and impractical ever designed.

Huge numbers of pikes were manufactured at the beginning of the Revolutionary Wars to arm the thousands of conscripts for whom no muskets were available; the weapon was archaic and largely useless and replaced as soon as possible. The lady illustrated (from a contemporary print entitled 'Jeune Française allant au Champ de Mars faire l'Exercise') wears the popular fashion (see Plate 34) of imitation military uniform, an expression of patriotism soon replaced by more conventional gowns. She is a civilian, but some redoubtable ladies actually served in the army. There are many accounts of women disguising themselves as men in order to follow a soldier-husband or sweetheart, but a few in this period fought as themselves. For example, the aristocratic Madame de Bennes joined the émigré Damas Legion in British service to fight 'in defence of her religion and her King', and was 'admired for the intrepid courage which always led her to the most dangerous post' (*London Chronicle*, 10 December 1795). Similarly, Royalist ladies fought in Charette's army, for example Mlle de Regrenil, who killed a republican hussar, took his horse and weapons and joined the Royalist cavalry.

21 BRITAIN:
a) Officer, Royal Artillery, campaign dress, 1794.
b) Civilian driver, Royal Artillery, 1793.
c) Gunner, Royal Artillery, 1792.

The gunner (after Dayes) shows Royal Artillery uniform at the outset of the Revolutionary wars: infantry style, blue with red facings and yellow lace (officers' gold). Regimental features include the white cartridge-box with brass crown badge on red cloth backing, the hammer and vent-picker affixed to the belt, and powder-flask slung over the shoulder. The uniform followed that of the infantry, the hat gradually becoming larger until replaced by the shako in 1800.

On active service (and at home) it was usual to wear a 'round hat' with yellow band and cockade-loop and (sometimes) red tuft. The shape of these hats is variously depicted, sometimes narrowing towards the top, with broad or narrow brim. Exactly when the hat was introduced is in doubt; campaign-sketches show it in the Netherlands in 1794, though General Mercer saw the bicorn in common use in 1797. De Loutherberg shows a different type of officer's head-dress in his picture, 'The Siege of Valenciennes', and in a sketch of Col. Congreve; a fur-crested 'round hat' with three gold lines around, worn with an unlaced coat which still had a 'turn-down' collar. Overalls were also used on campaign. De Loutherberg shows a mounted officer with white sheepskin shabraque and black fur holster-covers.

The knapsack shown by Dayes had a red-edged, blue-painted disc bearing a yellow-and-red crown with RA below, and below that —— BATTN. The civilian driver (on whom the artillery had to rely prior to the formation of a military corps of drivers) wears the typical 'round hat' (named 'Mother Shipton' by

Mercer after the noted Yorkshire witch), with a civilian carter's smock, though one battery inspection of 1798 notes a more 'military' style, the white smocks having blue collar and cuffs. As civilians they were armed only with a whip.

22 BRITAIN:
a) Officer,
2nd Dragoon Guards, 1797.
b) Officer,
3rd Dragoon Guards, 1790.

British heavy cavalry uniform developed like that of the infantry, collars becoming upright; and after 1796 closed to the waist with facing-coloured lapels sometimes persisting, and skirts 'cut so as to clear the seat when on horseback'. The 3rd Dragoon Guards officer (from a contemporary portrait) has an unusual collar, in which the collar-button appears to be in the lapel. The epaulettes bear the Prince of Wales' badge repeated on the shoulder-belt plate; by the 1796 regulations these were replaced by 'shoulder straps, of the colour of the facing of the regiment, with red wings, edged with white cloth, and laced and inter-lined with iron or brass plates, of sufficient strength to resist the cut of a sword . . .', but the officers of some regiments apparently retained their old epaulettes, judging from the British Military Library prints of c.1799, from which the 2nd D.G. officer is in part taken.

This figure has the closed lapels of 1796, with pouch-belt and waist-belt for the sword, replacing the earlier shoulder-belt. For this regiment there exists a complete 'Standing Orders' of 1795, most of which would have applied after the 1796 changes. The following extracts are applicable to the figure illustrated: 'All Officers . . . must wear the plain regimental hat and feather . . . on no account is an Officer to wear his hat over the back of his head. They must always wear a black velvet stock, and an exact regimental club and rosette, tied close to the head; the rosette black and clean, like those of the men. No boots must be worn but the exact regimental

[presumably the low riding-boots shown by the British Military Library] . . . when Officers are off duty, they may be worn pushed down . . . on any duty on foot . . . the silver-laced hat and feather, sash, and sword-belt over the coat . . . for a field day on horse-back . . . regimental spurs, broad swords, and plain hats . . . the sash . . . must go twice round the waist, and tie in the front, the ends hanging nearly half way down the thigh. . . . All hats and caps must be worn well forward upon the face, and over the right eye . . . the feathers must be . . . quite clean and white. . . .'

The last remark suggests that all-white feathers may have been worn, not the usual white-over-red shown by the British Military Library. A new sabre was introduced in 1796, a broad-bladed, disc-hilted and cumbersome weapon copied from Austrian designs; prior to this date the 1788 pattern—or variations of it—were used, a clumsy sword with half-basket hilt.

Facing-colours for heavy cavalry were as follows: 1st (King's) and 4th Dragoon Guards, 1st (Royal), 2nd (North British), 3rd (King's) and 5th (Royal Irish) Dragoons blue; 2nd (Queen's) and 7th D.G. black; 3rd and 6th D.G. white; 5th (Royal Irish) D.G. and 4th (Queen's) Dragoons green; 6th (Inniskilling) Dragoons yellow. Gold lace (yellow for other ranks) for the 1st, 3rd, 5th and 7th D.G., 1st, 2nd and 3rd Dragoons, and silver (white) for the remainder (white for O.R.s of the 1st Dragoons). The 5th Dragoons were disbanded in 1798.

23 BRITAIN:
a) Sergeant,
10th Light Dragoons, 1793.
b) Trumpeter,
10th Light Dragoons,
dismounted dress, 1793.

British light dragoons wore two garments—a sleeved waistcoat with braided breast, and a sleeveless 'shell' with small wings; both were dark blue, introduced in 1784 and replaced in 1796 by a dolman. The waistcoat had facing-coloured collar and cuffs and could be worn without the 'shell'; as early as 1790 the commanding officer of the 19th Light Dragoons was urging the replacement of the 'shell', being 'so little worn . . . that it is almost useless . . .'. The 'shell', which had a coloured collar, fastened across the breast with loops of braid, but usually only the upper pair of loops was fastened, the remainder being hooked crosswise to the upper or lower buttons of each pair, producing an X-shaped pattern. Wings were officially blue, but some units (despite official protests) wore facing-coloured wings until forbidden: the 11th (1789–90) and 16th (1789), at which date the 10th had 'fore-flaps of upper jacket lined with yellow instead of white'.

Officers' uniforms were different, the 'shell' having sleeves; some officers (as shown in a portrait of the 7th by Richard Arnold) having metal shoulder-scales instead of wings. In the early 1790s pelisse-like garments are shown, non-regulation and perhaps the 'shell' with fur trimming; certainly the officers of the 16th had leopardskin linings from 1785 until at least 1788. Rank-marking consisted of 'gold or silver looping' plus blue-and-facing-coloured sash for sergeants, and 'gold or silver cord around the collar and cuff' for corporals, but Stubbs' picture shows the 10th with rank-chevrons as well.

The helmet was the leather, fur-crested 'Tarleton' with cloth turban and plume of the facing-colour; by the mid-1790s plumes were becoming standard at white-over-red and turbans black, but the latter in the facing-colour persisted for years in some regiments. Regimental badges were worn on the right of the helmet, for example a rose, thistle and shamrock (9th), Prince of Wales' plumes (10th) and crossed bones over a skull (17th); others had crowned-Garter badges. Legwear (leather or plush breeches and boots when mounted; breeches, stockings and half-gaiters on foot) also had regimental variations; for example Robert Dighton shows Lt. Col. Affleck of the 16th (c. 1795–1801) in blue breeches. Horse-furniture was regimentally-coloured, as illustrated, though in 1789 the 10th had 'housings'

'like that of the Heavy Dragoons', and i 1792 the 8th had goatskin horse-furnitur Bayonets were issued, but not always mad use of; the sabre was the 1788 stirrup-hilte version worn from a shoulder-belt (except fc the 11th in 1789 who left theirs on 'horse back'), but regimental variations ar recorded.

Trumpeters usually wore 'reversed co ours', i.e. the colour of the regimental facing Stubbs showing a magnificent trumpeter c the 10th complete with fringed lace, ornat shoulder-belt and the squarish fur cap author ized in 1792.

Facing-colours were white (7th, 17th 18th), red (8th, 15th, 16th), buff (9th, 11th 12th, 13th), yellow (10th, 19th) and orang (14th); all had white lace (officers' silve except the 13th (yellow/gold). New regimen from 1792 were the 20th (yellow facings, silve lace), 21st (yellow/gold), 22nd (red/gold 23rd and 24th (light yellow/silver), 25th (red 26th (originally green, later blue or purple 27th (white), 28th (yellow) and 29th (buff and the 30th to 33rd about whose unifor little is known. Some were supposed to hav had red uniforms (including the 22nd, 24t and 25th) but these were never adopted, reg ments pre-empting the regulations by makin up blue ones before the order for red. Othe were given grey jackets, the colour used fc tropical service: 19th, 20th, 24th, 25th, 27t and 28th for example; though a counter-orde specified blue at least the 25th made up th grey and were allowed to wear them. Thos serving in the tropics wore a variety of tropic helmets, including a magnificent, red-mane crested helmet by the 20th.

24 BRITAIN:
  a) Drummer,
  Buckinghamshire Militia,
  1793.
  b) Grenadier,
  Buckinghamshire Militia,
  1793.

The Militia was a statutory home-defenc

force of county infantry battalions, raised by ballot rather than true 'conscription', as a balloted man could buy exemption by paying a 'substitute' to serve in his place. The Militia's real value was in relieving regular troops from garrison duty, serving as a defence against invasion and, more importantly in the strife-ridden mid-1790s, maintaining civil order, in which unsavoury duty the Militia was supported by the volunteers and yeomanry (see Plates 25, 33 and 34).

Militia wore infantry uniform with regimental distinctions, the figures illustrated taken from drawings by Sir William Young, Bt, of the Buckinghamshire Militia. The grenadier uniform includes laced wings and brass match-case and a most unusual cap, apparently a brass-fitted leather mitre with fur rear portion. The drummer's cap apparently has back- and front-plates of leather in the style of a light infantry cap, with fur between the plates, and what is probably intended on the original to represent a facing-coloured turban. The design of front-plate is unclear but may be a scroll-shaped device; the yellow wings and laced sleeves are other musicians' distinctions.

Battalion companies are shown with plain red wings edged white—minus the fringe and lace-design of the grenadier—and bicorns with red-over-white plume (red-over-white-over-red for the sergeant major). A Grenadier officer is shown in an old-style fur cap with gilt plate, and musicians' uniform like that of the drummer except for a bicorn with red feather edging and red-over-white plume. The drum major's hat was similar with silver lace, his coat yellow with red facings, and his baldric black with silver lace. The battalion's Negro musicians wore fanciful dress of yellow short jacket with red collar, cuffs and wings, mixed red-and-white lace and half-sleeves, over a white sleeved waistcoat and gaiter-trousers with red ankle-boots, and either a white turban with yellow-over-black plume, or a black peakless 'stovepipe' cap with yellow turban and silver cords and semi-circular plate.

25 BRITAIN:
a) **Sergeant Major,**
Royal Edinburgh Volunteers,
1795.
b) **Officer,**
Royal Huddersfield Fusiliers,
1796.

The Volunteers were a 'home guard' of small local companies, volunteering to serve in their own locality against foreign invasion or the much more likely event of civil disorder, often providing their own arms and equipment and many serving without the pay due to them for every attendance, drilling for several hours a week and available to be called to arms at a moment's notice by the local magistrate or area commander. Severe riots, often with bloodshed, were common in the mid-1790s. Only in the expanded 1803–04 volunteer force was widespread social balance achieved, the earlier companies frequently composed exclusively of gentry or middle-class.

Some volunteer corps wore infantry uniform, distinguished only by insignia from that of the regulars, for example the Huddersfield Volunteers illustrated, raised in 1794 by a local subscription of £1,440 5s. By 1798 the title 'Royal Huddersfield Fusiliers' had been adopted and the four companies (total 232 men) agreed to serve in 'any part of the kingdom' in the event of invasion. A subsidiary corps raised for the protection of the immediate locality in 1798, the Huddersfield Armed Association, wore blue uniform with scarlet collar and cuffs and a 'round hat'.

Blue uniforms were common at this period, often rich in ornamentation, so expensive as to preclude many from becoming volunteers. The Royal Edinburgh Volunteers, ten companies strong (including two of grenadiers) were raised in October 1794. Their uniform (that illustrated from a portrait of Sergeant Major Gould by George Watson) included blue coat with scarlet collar and cuff-flaps; an extant example has half-lapels. All ranks apparently wore epaulettes, an extant pair being a gold-edged shoulder-strap with thin gold fringe. The head-dress was a 'round hat' with two black and one white plume, and a bearskin crest for grenadiers, who had grenade-badges on their turnbacks. Equipment was black leather, later painted white; the paint began to shell off, giving a piebald appearance, which necessitated a new issue of buff-leather. The belt-plate was engraved with the title ROYAL EDINBURGH over an anchor, over the City arms, over VOLUNTEERS. Gould is shown with an officer-pattern sash and sword, the latter common amongst all officers, the elegant 'spadroon'.

'Volunteer fever'—largely a spontaneous burst of patriotism—was widespread; those interested in an account of their reaction to a false invasion-alarm, written by a volunteer, should read Sir Walter Scott's *The Antiquary*. This patriotism can be seen in the lists, compiled by parish constables, of all able-bodied men willing to serve if invasion came. For example, here are some remarks by inhabitants of Slaithwaite, near Huddersfield, where 279 men out of 574 volunteered: John Ramsden, engineer: 'No objection to be enrowled (sic) in the Infantry, provided they be trained at Slaithwaite'; Joel Hoyle, clothier: 'hath no implements (but) will work hard'; Samuel Wood, butcher: 'Will furnish himself with arms and stand up for the defence of the town'; James Sykes of Cophill: 'determined to kill a Frenchman, if possible'. The constable recorded just one dissenter, another James Sykes, who 'will assist all in his power for the French to have their own', and, added the constable, 'Consequently he must be a *Jacobin!*'

26 SWITZERLAND/BRITAIN:
   a) SWITZERLAND: Commandant, Basle Dragoons, 1793.
   b) BRITAIN: Officer, Roverea's Regt, 1800.

The officer of the Basle Dragoons is taken from a portrait of Major Daniel Merian by Franz Feyerabend, the unit being part of the Basle contingent of the forces of the Swiss Confederation. The horse-furniture for all ranks comprised a square-cut red shabraque with white edge, blue circular valise, and blue holster-caps with white edging and a white-edged red disc in the centre. An archaic feature of this unit was a mounted drummer who carried a side-drum slung on his left side; his uniform was white with red chevrons on the sleeves and red facings.

Following French occupation, the remnants of the Swiss forces were formed into three large units (Regts Roverea, Bachmann and Salis) and three smaller (Regts Courten and Paraviccini and the Légion de Managhalta) in British pay, though serving with the Austrians. They provided the foundation of the excellent British Swiss corps of the Napoleonic Wars (see Plate 50). Their uniform is variously shown in contemporary prints: Bachmann has a single-breasted sky-blue jacket faced black, sky-blue breeches and Austrian 'round hat' with oval brass plate bearing B; later the uniform apparently became green with red facings and a cylindrical shako with yellow lace bands and black-over-yellow plume; the jägers had green shako-lace and feather. Roverea is shown with black-faced green uniform and light blue breeches, green turnbacks edged black (other regiments had facing-coloured turnbacks); Martinet shows the shako with yellow lace and cords, red cockade and white plume for grenadiers, green for jägers and black for musketeers; another print shows the shako with white band around the base, red and yellow cockade and yellow-over-black plume, the officer as illustrated. The red arm-band was said to be peculiar to Roverea, but one officer claimed that all Swiss in British pay had red brassards with white cross. Salis wore a similar uniform with plain shako, the jägers having leopardskin shako-band and green feather; Courten may have worn the same as Roverea with yellow facings. In all cases, officers wore long-skirted coats and the men jackets; equipment white, and black for jägers.

27 BRITAIN:
a) **Private, York Rangers, 1794.**
b) **Musician, York Rangers, 1794.**
c) **Private, Regt Royal Louis, 1794.**

The emigration of thousands of middle class and gentry from France provided a rich fund of recruits for the nations aligned against the republicans, many such recruits having a personal interest in the restoration of the monarchy. Three 'armies' (little more than 5,000 strong) were formed exclusively of émigrés, those of the Princes of Bourbon, disbanded after the 1792 campaign, and the Prince de Condé, passing from Austrian to Russian service. Other émigrés went into Spanish, Swedish and Sardinian service, and a large number into British. The latter usually wore British-style uniform, with their own distinctions; they varied in quality from superb to scurvy units of ex-prisoners. The émigrés were harshly treated; many of those surviving the Netherlands campaign and the Quiberon débâcle were sent to die of disease in the West Indies.

'Royal Louis' was a line regiment in British pay raised in the name of Louis XVII in 1793 for the defence of Toulon, from where it covered the evacuation and was the last to embark. In Hood's expedition to Corsica it received great praise (from Nelson among others) but on reaching England was drafted into Hervilly's Regt after great protest. The uniform was that of a French line regiment, complete with white cockade; grenadiers' fur caps had brass plates bearing a fleur-de-lys, white cords, red rear patch bearing a white cross, and red feather; they had red epaulettes and turnback-grenades. Musicians wore the French royal livery—blue coat faced red, with red-and-white lace.

The York Rangers (or Chasseurs), named after the Duke of York, was a rifle corps formed to supplement Britain's meagre supply of experienced light infantry, the officers largely French and many of the other

ranks German. It served with distinction in the Netherlands but was sent to its end in the West Indies in 1796. The leather light infantry cap had a fox's brush over the crown (sometimes front-to-back), sometimes shown with a star-over-scroll badge. The musicians' first uniform was the single-breasted jacket illustrated; a later version retained the colouring but had lapels like the private's, with wings as before. Several contemporary drawings show officers with single-breasted jackets, blue with yellow facings and wings like the musician's, sometimes with yellow lace bands on the cap, and red-over-green plume. The bottom of the waistcoat protruded below the jacket-waist. The unit's artillery company apparently wore the same uniform with red collar and cuffs, one officer shown with brown overalls with wide yellow stripes.

28 BRITAIN:
a) **Grenadier, Loyal Emigrants, 1796.**
b) **Private, Regt Béon, 1795.**
c) **Grenadier, Regt Castries, 1796.**

The best émigré corps was the Loyal Emigrants, raised in England and by 1794 1,264 strong, in two battalions. Composed almost entirely of French nobility, it served with the greatest distinction. The original uniform was of British infantry style, red with yellow facings, white loops in pairs with one black and two red stripes, yellow shoulder-straps edged white, white-laced bicorn with either white or black plume; Hamilton Smith shows an unlaced hat and yellow half-lapels. Later, perhaps when sent to Portugal, the shorter-skirted coat illustrated was worn; chasseurs had green hat-lace and plume, white-laced yellow wings with chain strap edged green, and a red waistcoat with lace loops. For all except grenadiers the belt-plate was oval, bearing the Royal arms and title. Officers' lace is described as either silver or gold. The unit's veteran company was aged between 65 and 75; they were begged to retire at Quiberon, but as

M. Faulte de Vanteaux (aged 65 and serving in the ranks as 'fourrier') said, 'Do you think that the Veterans are incapable of fighting and dying?'; only 45 out of 120 survived. Only 97 members of the unit escaped from Quiberon, the remainder either killed or taken prisoner and, like all captured émigrés, summarily executed. The Loyal Emigrants was disbanded in 1802.

The Béon Legion was raised for Dutch service, transferring to British in 1795; after fighting to the end at Quiberon the remnants were broken up amongst other units, including the Loyal Emigrants. The uniform illustrated was that worn in Dutch service, some sources indicating orange facings (which may have appeared red). Hamilton Smith's uncoloured sketch shows wings and an upright 'round hat' with feather. The Hussars of the Béon Legion wore light blue with red collar and cuffs, white braid, black pelisse-fur, peakless shako with white cords and lace, light blue sabretache with white edging and crowned GR device. Hamilton Smith shows the same, excepting a light blue mirliton. Horse-furniture was a white sheepskin, with or without light blue shabraque with yellow vandyke edge.

Regt de Castries was formed in Holland in 1794, wearing a simple red single-breasted jacket faced light green with white lace, and 'round hat' with red turban and white plume, later with bearskin crest which the Duc de Castries was authorized to purchase at 3/- each. When the unit went to Portugal the uniform illustrated was probably worn, here with grenadiers' hat-badge and epaulettes; the belt-plate bore a fleur-de-lys. Hamilton Smith shows green half-lapels and turnbacks with bicorn and white feather; but it seems that clothing may not always have been uniform, as an extant letter notes that '2,000 infantry suits will immediately be wanted for Regiments Castries and Mortemart, if they have black and green collars and cuffs so much the better', which implies that, typically, whatever was available was used, despite regulations. The unit retained its white (Bourbon) cockade until 1801, when it was ordered to adopt the black British cockade; this was partly evaded by placing a black cockade in the centre of a white one, thus maintaining the unit's visible support for the French monarchy.

29 RUSSIA:
a) N.C.O,
Duke of Bourbon's Grenadiers,
Armée de Condé,
with flag, 1799.
b) Cossack, 1799.

Russian uniform was adopted by the émigré 'Armée de Condé' when it entered that country's service in 1797, with distinctive black facings. Bicorn hats were worn by all save grenadiers, who wore brass-fronted mitre caps, with the design enamelled in 'some Russian regiments. This uniform was a reversion of the pre-1786 uniform; the 1786–96 uniform (attempting to provide a more functional costume) included short jacket, overalls and a curious leather cap (see *Military Uniforms of the World*, Fig. 147).

One of three Condé infantry regiments, the Duke of Bourbon's Grenadiers wore the mitre with red headband bearing brass grenades, and a yellow cloth back with yellow-and-black piping and pompom. The yellow lace had a red stripe and red-and-yellow tassel; ordinary infantry equipment included black leather cartridge-boxes with circular brass plates embossed with the double-eagle, and four small grenades in the corners; sword-knots were white for the 1st Btn, 2nd orange, 3rd black, 4th dark blue and 5th red. Prussian muskets with red slings were carried. N.C.O rank-distinctions included gold lace and black-and-white sword-knot. The other Condé infantry units, the Hohenlohe-Durant Musketeers and the Régt Noble à Pied wore the standard green infantry uniform with red turnbacks and the black Condé facings, the latter unit having pointed yellow lace loops on the lapels, pale yellow waistcoat and breeches. Grenadier-caps of the Hohenlohe-Durant had white metal plates, dark green headband with white grenades, dark green rear and yellow-

and-black piping and pompom. Both cavalry regiments (Régt Noble à Cheval and Dragons d'Enghien) also wore dark green with black facings and bicorns.

Each infantry regiment carried ten flags, nine 'coloured' and one 'white' in the manner of Russian regiments; the design comprised the double-eagle on an orange disc, with a coloured background and contrasting diagonal 'rays'; all proclaimed their Bourbon allegiance by the white cross and fleurs-de-lys in each corner (see black and white Plate E). Colouring:

Regt	'White' flag		'Coloured' flags	
	Field	Rays	Field	Rays
Noble	White	Black	Black	White
Grens. de B.	White	Orange	Orange	Red
Hohenlohe	White	Dark Blue	Black	Dark Blue

The cossacks, originally nomadic steppe-dwellers, were the best irregular cavalry in Europe, a fact often belied by their appearance: fur or cloth cap, loose jacket or kaftan, baggy trousers and boots, plus an accumulation of looted, stolen or captured weapons to supplement their 'native' swords, pistol and lance. Their mounts, small, rough, ill-conditioned ponies, were equally unprepossessing but like their riders were incredibly resilient and resourceful. Horse-furniture was often no more than a folded blanket and rope bridle. The figure illustrated is after von Kobell, who shows the widespread use of checked trousers; more extensive details on these feared tribesmen can be found in *Uniforms of the Retreat from Moscow*.

30 FRANCE:
a) Volunteer, Army of the Rhine, 1796.
b) Officer with Colour, 5th Demi-Brigade de Bataille, 1796.

The ragged infantryman is taken from an eye-witness drawing of October 1796 (by Benjamin Zix), an evocative figure dressed like a scarecrow but, in the original, loaded with plunder and a bulging purse. The neck-cloth and waistcoat are civilian; tattered legwear

was the rule rather than the exception in the German and Italian campaigns of this period.

The flags of the early Revolutionary period had little standardization, mostly red, white and blue and bearing political symbols such as fasces or Phrygian cap. Regimental and battalion identification was usual, and latterly battle-honours were added. The complexity of designs was confused further by amalgamations; for example the 88th Demi-Brigade carried the flags of the earlier 112th and 173rd. An attempt at standardization was made in 1797, when units in Italy received a standard design (see black and white Plate D). 'Tricolor' cravats or streamers were usually hung from the top of the pole, which was often black or painted in red, white and blue spirals. The 1797 flag was 160 cm square, but earlier versions varied in size.

31 BRITAIN:
a) Admiral, Royal Navy, 1794 (Lord Howe).
b) Seaman, Royal Navy.

Naval officers' uniform was styled like that of the army, the one illustrated taken from Mather Brown's painting of the Battle of the First of June, showing the 1787 uniform for flag officers, with gold-laced hat and lapel-less coat; a mixed blue-and-gold cord ran around the crown of the hat, its two tassels sometimes visible at the ends of the hat. A feature of Mosnier's painting of Lord Rodney, wearing the same uniform, is a narrow gold cord on the right shoulder, added unofficially to retain the riband of the Order of the Bath. White-lapelled coats were worn by lower-ranking officers, the 1795 regulations changing lapels to blue to be worn by all ranks. Hitherto, rank-marking had been in the amount of gold lace on the coat; gold epaulettes were introduced in 1795, bearing three silver stars for Admiral, Vice-Admiral two, Rear-Admiral one; captains of three years' standing had two plain epaulettes, captains of junior rank an epaulette on the right and commanders one on the left; lower ranks had no epaulettes. From 1795 it was common to have the lapels closed to the waist, and unlaced 'undress' uniforms were usually worn in action. The hat grew progressively larger and it became customary for all except flag officers to wear it 'fore-and-after' instead of crossways as before. Dress-regulations were frequently ignored, however; in 1797 Earl St Vincent issued an order deploring the appearance of officers who 'dressed like shop-keepers in coloured cloaths, and others wearing Round Hats'.

With no dress regulations for ordinary seamen, they wore common nautical dress. The 'round hat' was usually straw, often tarred like the 'queue'; the blue short jacket had an easily-opening 'mariner's cuff' to allow the sleeves to be rolled up, often with seams and edges bound with white tape, for strength as well as decoration, and as many brass buttons as the wearer could afford; loose, wide trousers to facilitate rolling-up; shoes and stockings were worn ashore but bare feet were usual aboard ship. The large neckerchief was worn around the head in action, and the waistcoat reserved for shore leave. Some captains attempted to introduce a degree of uniformity: in 1805, for example, the crew of HMS *Tribune* wore gold hat-bands emblazoned with the ship's name, blue-laced white waistcoats, blue jackets with three rows of brass buttons, and blue trousers.

32 BRITAIN:
a) Private,
42nd Highlanders,
campaign dress, 1794.
b) Officer,
Caithness & Rothsay
Fencibles, 1795.
c) Sergeant,
Sutherland Fencibles, 1795.

At this period Highland dress was midway between functional native costume and the fanciful travesty it became from the 1820s. The short jacket was of infantry style. The kilt and plaid were the 'breachan-an-fheilidh' or 'belted plaid', a stretch of tartan cloth worn around the waist and hooked up to the rear of the left shoulder, secured by a belt. Clan tar-

tans not yet having emerged, the 'Government' tartan (now known as 'Black Watch' was universal, with coloured overstripes fo some regiments. The Dayes picture on whic the 42nd Highlander is based includes a hai sporran, which was probably discarded o campaign. It was unusual for the hose to hav turned-over tops as shown by Dayes, straigh tops being more common. Dayes shows th broadsword; possibly his subject was a co poral, but the broadsword may have been ca ried by all ranks. The 42nd Highlander (Black Watch) had blue facings and whit 'bastion'-shaped lace with a red line, and earl in 1791 exchanged their black leather equip ment for white. Dayes shows a shoulder-strap

The Highland bonnet consisted of a blu cloth cap with coloured 'diced' border and re 'toorie' (pompom), with a few black feathers It was usual for the men to buy extra feather to enhance their appearance, as stated by th 42nd's 1790 Inspection Return: 'bonnets ar entirely disfigured, they are so covered wit lofty feathers that they appear like hig Grenadier caps of black bear-skin', and whe the 2/78th prepared to sail for South Africa i 1794 their sergeants were instructed 't deliver the Bonnets to the Qr Master Serjt . . and take a list of such Mens names as hav Feathers of their own, and the number the give in'; the traditional feather bonne developed from this unofficial adornment Trousers were worn occasionally, usuall white for tropical service, though as early a 1796 the 92nd in Corsica were ordered to con vert their plaids into 'truibhs' (trews), a order so unpopular that the kilt was resume In common with other infantry, fu grenadier-caps were worn for some time.

'Fencibles' were line regiments enlisted o condition that they were not eligible for over seas service unless they volunteered to go. Th contravention by the Government of the con ditions under which the Fencibles ha enlisted caused a number of 'mutinies' (i effect, token 'strikes') among some Scottis Fencible corps (the majority were raised i Scotland). Except for facing-colours, lace insignia and sometimes tartan, Fencible corp wore ordinary Highland uniform, several being recorded as wearing 'truibhs'.

The Sutherland Fencibles sergeant is based on a John Kay picture of the six-feet-ten-inch 'Big Sam' McDonald whose feats of strength (including the transport on one shoulder of a huge cannon) made him a legend; he was paid an extra 2/6d (12½p) a day to buy 'more sustenance than his military pay could afford', and owing to his height throwing the line out of symmetry was appointed to lead the regimental mascot (a stag) at the head of the regiment. Kay shows 'Big Sam' with a fully-feathered bonnet, but lacking the usual shoulder-sash worn by sergeants of Highland regiments. The Sutherland Fencibles were raised in 1793 and disbanded in 1799.

The Caithness and Rothsay were raised in 1794 and disappeared in 1802, being one of several Fencible corps to send detachments to Ireland before and during the ''98'. The uniform is shown in Sir Henry Raeburn's portrait of Sir John Sinclair of Ulbster Bt; the bonnet-plumes are not shown clearly by Raeburn, but a *British Military Journal* print shows the style illustrated. This was the only Highland corps to wear the sash around the waist, and Sinclair of Ulbster has 'truibhs' with fringed bottom and leather reinforcing; the colour of the tartan-overstripe is not clear from Raeburn but Kay's recruiting-card for the 2nd Btn shows it as yellow. The belt-plate was curious, bearing a crown over a thistle and, around the edges, CAITHNESS and FLODDEN FIELD, commemorating the last time the Caithness clansmen were called out for service!

33 BRITAIN:
a) Trooper,
St Mary (Islington)
Volunteer Cavalry, 1799.
b) Grenadier,
East Yorkshire Militia,
1797.

Volunteer cavalry or yeomanry were the equivalent of the infantry volunteers. The St Mary (Islington) troop (after Rowlandson) wears typical light cavalry uniform, copied from that of the regular light dragoons (after 1796, when the dolman replaced the waistcoat and 'shell' of Plate 23). Rowlandson notes that this 'respectable Corps of Cavalry' was the first to be raised in London, 'immediately after the Enemy presumed to land upon the Welch coast'; when the wife of the commanding officer, J. P. Anderdon, presented the troop's standard which she herself had provided (1799), her speech contained a typical verse: 'Remember still—they fight in Virtue's cause, Who guard their KING, their LIBERTY, and LAWS!' This sentiment was echoed by the troop motto: 'Dulce Est Pro Patria Mori', a genuine and creditable expression of patriotism at a time before Horace's words had been given a new slant by Wilfred Owen.

Sadly, the yeomanry's service was usually against its own countrymen, in an attempt to save life and property from civil disorder. Hunger and rising prices resulted in a multitude of incidents like the following abbreviated account from the London Chronicle, recounting how in August 1795 a hungry crowd in Barrow-upon-Soar seized a waggonload of corn and dragged it to the church, whereupon the magistrates '... and the Leicester troop of cavalry ... found a vast assemblage of people in the church-yard ... the Magistrates remonstrated with them ... unwilling to proceed to extremities, it was proposed that eight quarters of corn should be left, which was agreed to ... on their going off, however, the cavalry (who before had been insulted) were assailed with brick bats, and some shots fired upon them ... one of which wounded Mr. Stringer in the knee. The cavalry fired in return, and eleven victims fell; three were shot dead on the spot, and eight dangerously wounded ...'.

The East Yorkshire militiaman is taken from Scott's series of militia prints, and shows the flat-topped grenadier cap (also worn by some line regiments), unusual square-cut wings, one-piece 'gaiter-trousers' and a small grenade-badge above the usual shoulder-belt plate.

34 BRITAIN:
a) **Lady in 'uniform' of the Royal East India Company Volunteers, 1799.**
b) **Private, Bridge Ward Volunteers, 1799.**
c) **Private, Battalion Company, Birmingham Loyal Association, 1798.**

'Uniforms' (see Plate 20) were often worn by ladies whose husbands/brothers/fathers/fiancés were militia or volunteer officers, some really spectacular costumes being recorded, like that of the beautiful Lady Hester Stanhope, niece of William Pitt, who appeared at parades of her uncle's Cinque Ports Volunteers 'dressed "à l'amazone" in scarlet habit and a military hat perched on ash blond curls and a pair of gauntlets on her long aristocratic fingers'. The lady illustrated (from a contemporary painting) wears a typical costume, including 'round hat' and high-waisted jacket, in the colouring of London's largest and most proficient volunteer corps, the Royal East India Company Volunteers.

Rowlandson illustrates the unusual uniform of the Bridge Ward Volunteers, a sixty-strong company of the volunteer 'brigade' also including the Tower, Langbourne, Aldgate and Billingsgate Ward companies, forming the South-East District of Loyal London Volunteers. The company was raised in May 1798 'to serve in the City of London, for its internal Tranquility', with company H.Q. at Fishmongers' Hall. Rowlandson notes that the helmet-badge consisted of a crowned Garter with GR in the centre, the belt-plate bearing BWA (Bridge Ward Association), and the cartridge-box 'Star, Garter and Crown'.

The Birmingham Loyal Association (raised 1797) performed the usual duties plus (as did a number of volunteer corps) acting as amateur firemen. The uniform shown is from an engraving by E. Rudge; the battalion company uniform is illustrated, the flank companies having dark blue wings with gold edging and fringe, the grenadiers large fur caps with black-enamelled brass plate, white cords and white-over-red plume, and the light company a 'Tarleton' helmet with leopardskin turban and white-over-red plume. As might be expected from a unit in which Matthew Boulton was implicated, their regimental medals were amongst the finest works of art of the age.

35 BRITAIN:
a) **Officer, Light Company, 12th Foot, 1796.**
b) **Private, 5th Btn, 60th Foot, 1799.**

Before whole battalions were transformed into the vital light infantry rôle, Britain depended upon mercenaries and regimental 'light companies' of line regiments. The latter's functional uniform, evolved in the American War, had become progressively more fancy, with useless leather caps which had to be tied on. To increase functionality, the 'round hat' was widely adopted, which together with the short-tailed jacket and sometimes different weapons (light muskets and even tomahawks) presented a totally different appearance to the ordinary companies. The uniform of the 12th illustrated was described by a company officer, George Elers (1796):

'My outfit cost me £300 . . . I had six regimental jackets . . . shirts about twelve dozen, and everything in the same proportion . . . appointed to the light company, I was obliged to send up to London for a sabre and wings instead of epaulettes, and lots of narrow gold lace for my scarlet waistcoat. We bore blue pantaloons edged with scarlet, hats covered over with the finest black ostrich feathers, and a stand-up feather composed of black and red. They looked very handsome, but were expensive . . . a good shower of rain soon took their smartness off.'

The sabres mentioned were usually carried by 'flank' company officers in preference to the straight-bladed sword; there was no regulation pattern until 1803 but they usually followed the same, barred-hilted pattern. Other ranks' uniform included bearskin hat-crests and 'bastion'-shaped loops in pairs; the officer illustrated has no lace loops but embroidery instead.

The 60th (Royal American) Regt provided the first 'rifle' battalions of the British army, light infantry armed with rifled muskets in the manner of German Jägers; in fact both battalions were largely German in composition, both with dark green uniforms, the forerunners of the Rifle Corps (ultimately numbered 95th) whose exploits became legend during the Peninsular War. The uniform of the 5/60th well illustrates the description of a 'foreign looking battalion' described by the *Gentleman's Magazine* in 1799. The shako, slightly wider at the top, preceded the general introduction of the cap and bore the bugle-horn badge made famous by the 95th. Some sources show a single shoulder-belt and waist-belt, others cross-belts; probably both styles were used at some period. Powder-horns on a flask-cord attached to the shoulder-belt were worn by all who carried the rifle; before the adoption of the famous 'Baker' it is likely that several types of German hunting-rifle would be used, with brass-hilted sword-bayonet. Officers *may* have worn the 'Tarleton', though a miniature of Lieut. Woolf showing this helmet may represent an émigré uniform. The 6th Btn 60th had a similar uniform, but with green shako-cords, green jacket with green collar, cuffs, turn-backs and shoulder-straps all piped red, the shoulder-straps ending in black worsted tufts, and white breeches; black leather equipment for both battalions. Clothing Regulations of 1802 note that the jackets of the 6th Btn (and the rifle companies of the 60th's other battalions, who otherwise wore red infantry uniform faced blue) were made without turn-backs, 'but cut to slope off behind', with 'back skirts to fold well over between the hip buttons'.

36 AUSTRIA:
a) **Fusilier officer,**
4th Regt, 1799.
b) **Fusilier,**
41st Regt, 1800.
c) **Grenadier,**
33rd (Hungarian) Regt, 1800.

In 1798 the Austrian infantry uniform was altered, the jacket gradually becoming neater and, most noticeably, the leather cap being replaced by a brass-fitted 'classical' leather helmet with black-over-yellow crest, not always the neat, smart item often depicted, extant examples being heavy and cumbersome. The large brass front-plate bore the Imperial cypher FII. Officers retained long-tailed coats, the presence or absence of coloured turnbacks apparently varying between regiments. They wore the usual, heavily-tasselled, gold-and-black sash and, on campaign, frequently an open-topped pistol-holster on shoulder-belt, with a narrow shoulder-strap sometimes being added to the coat to retain it, and a dark grey frock-coat. Other ranks' helmets were less ornate and sometimes smaller, and their gaiters now extended only to below the knee. New equipment replaced the shoulder-knapsack shown in Plate 15, the hide pack now worn on the back with the grey greatcoat rolled above, with cartridge-box and leather-framed canteen as before. Grenadiers' fur caps retained the brass plate and padded rear section, which was striped in 'wavy'-edged lace; the colouring of the cloth rear varied, some authorities claiming a universal design but contemporary pictures suggesting that the facing-colour was usually incorporated; peaks to the grenadier caps were not universal at this date. The sabre was discontinued for fusiliers in 1798, but retained by grenadiers, whose brass bursting-grenade cartridge-box badges were a further distinction. 'Hungarian' regiments were distinguished by tight light blue breeches with mixed black-and-yellow lace on seam and thigh-knots, ankle-boots, and the so-called 'bear-paw' lace loop with fringe worn on their pointed cuffs. Hungarian officers

—even those of fusilier companies—often carried sabres. The sprig of oak-leaves in the cap was worn by most Austrian troops.

37 AUSTRIA:
a) Officer.
Light Infantry, 1800.
b) Private,
Border Infantry, 1799.
c) Private,
Lower Austrian State Corps, 1797.

The Austrian light infantry (of which fifteen battalions were formed in 1798 and disbanded in 1801) wore infantry uniform and equipment (with sabres), of distinctive light grey colouring, with short-tailed jackets worn by both officers and men. Both pointed 'Hungarian' cuffs (sometimes depicted without lace) and round 'German' cuffs were worn; the infantry helmet had separate brass letters, FII, in place of the front-plate.

The 'Grenz-Infanterie' (Border or Frontier troops), adept at marksmanship and skirmishing, wore 'Hungarian'-style uniform with tall cylindrical cap, to which a peak was added in 1798. Over the brown uniform the man illustrated wears his caped cloak, a feature peculiar to Border infantry, instead of the greatcoat. Equipment included a canvas haversack, often carried in lieu of the ordinary knapsack.

Amongst the 'irregulars' of the Imperial army were six corps of Viennese Volunteers, totalling some 37,000. Each corps was drawn from a particular social background, the one illustrated consisting of nobility and state officials; others comprised students, middle-class, merchants, etc. All wore the 'pike-grey' jacket illustrated, the cockade and plume in provincial colouring (here, Lower Austria). All members wore silver epaulettes.

38 FRANCE/POLAND:
a) FRANCE: Lancer,
Polish Danube Legion, 1799–1800.
b) POLAND: 'Scytheman',
Kosciusko's Army, 1794.

The 'scytheman' illustrated belongs not to the Revolutionary Wars proper but to the Polish rebellion against the Prusso-Russian domination imposed by the Second Partition of Poland (1793). Thaddeus Kosciusko, whose service in the American War of Independence inspired his democratic ideas, led an army composed initially of peasants with some army support, winning a victory over Russian occupation forces at Raclawice (3 April 1794). The Poles successfully defended Warsaw but lack of co-ordination led to a crushing defeat by Russia at Maciejowice (10 October 1794) in which Kosciusko was captured. The rebellion collapsed and the Third Partition (1795) wiped the Polish state off the map.

Kosciusko's valiant peasant troops, armed with axes, pikes and scythes, wore civilian dress, contemporary pictures showing wide-brimmed 'round hats' or, as illustrated, the square-topped 'konfederatka', the forerunner of the 'czapka' adopted by lancers throughout Europe.

Emigration following the Third Partition provided a fund of recruits for French and French-satellite armies, culminating with the founding of the Duchy of Warsaw which supplied many thousands of troops to Napoleon's 'Grande Armée'. The Danube Legion, comprising lancers, hussars, infantry and artillery, was formed in 1799 and served in Italy; the uniform illustrated, after Hoffman, is typical 'lancer' dress including the traditional 'czapka' (shown by Hoffman with monumental proportions, probably an exaggeration, and apparently with a six-sided top). The 'kurtka' lancer-jacket with short tails and 'plastron' front, and the lance, a traditional Polish weapon were used to great effect in the Napoleonic Wars, the lance being so closely linked to Poland that when other nations formed corps of lancers they almost invariably wore Polish costume.

39 BATAVIAN REPUBLIC/MODENA:
a) BATAVIAN REPUBLIC:
Grenadier,
2nd Demi-Brigade, 1797.
b) MODENA: Musician,
National Guard, 1798.
c) MODENA: Grenadier,
National Guard, 1798.

Like most French satellite states, the Batavian Republic's army wore French-style uniform, apparently with higher collar, longer coat-tails and larger hat than the French pattern. Company-distinctions were like those of the French, facing-colours (borne on collar, lapels and cuffs) being red for the 1st Demi-Brigade, 2nd crimson, 3rd and 4th white, 5th and 6th light blue, 7th Demi-Brigade and Regt Waldeck yellow, and Regt Sachsen-Gotha red; red turnbacks for 1st and 4th and Regt Sachsen-Gotha; 2nd, 3rd and 6th white, 4th light blue, 7th and Regt Waldeck yellow; red piping for 4th and Regt Sachsen-Gotha and white for the remainder. The 4th had a red collar piped white. Black cockades replaced the previous orange.

The Modena National Guard uniforms are taken from contemporary sketches by Canon Rovatti of Modena, recorded by Messrs Crociani and Brandani in 'Tradition'. The grenadier wears a cap formerly belonging to the Duke of Modena's Grenadiers, re-issued to the town militia. The light company wore a similar dress with green epaulettes and sword-knot, and a curious black leather cap with white metal plate embossed LE over BM—perhaps signifying 'Liberta Eguaglianza' (Liberty, Equality) and 'Battalglione Modenese'; a yellow hair mane and upright green plume completed the head-dress. The artillery company wore a similar uniform, with red epaulettes, sword-knot and waistcoat, and bicorn like the musician with red lace 'ties' and plume.

40 RUSSIA;
a) Infantryman,
campaign dress, 1799.
b) Conscript, 1799.
c) Infantryman,
campaign dress, 1799.

Despite the smartening-up process imposed by Czar Paul I, a rare view of the Russian army's campaign dress is given by von Kobell's picture of Suvarov's army in Italy and Switzerland. Gone is the pipeclay and powdered hair, simple uniform with a minimum of equipment being worn. Probably this represents the day-to-day dress of the Russian army on active service, not the mannikin-like figures portrayed by later artists. Von Kobell also shows a motley collection of conscripted recruits, a few with accoutrements and most with muskets (with which they look distinctly unfamiliar); all wear civilian clothes, with cloth or fur hats, jackets or kaftans, baggy trousers and high boots. Nevertheless, the ornate full dress (Plate 29) *was* worn on campaign at times, Surtees noting during the Helder expedition: '. . . their riflemen were shod with boots very much resembling those of our fishermen, coming up considerably higher than the knee; thus rendering them . . . incapable of celerity of movement . . . their grenadiers were dressed more apropos, having high sugar-loaf shaped caps, mounted with a great deal of brass, and projecting forward at the top, with long coats, and gaiters reaching above the knees . . .'.

Russian infantry facing-colours were determined by the 'Inspection' or district to which the regiment was allocated. These colours were: Brest lemon-yellow, Crimea 'natural' (buff), Finland yellow, Lithuania light green, Moscow orange, St Petersburg red, Ukraine rose-pink, Caucasus medium blue, Dniester lilac, Kiev raspberry-red, Livonia sky-blue, Orenburg brown, Smolensk grey.

113

41 FRANCE/IRELAND:
a) **FRANCE: Ensign,**
Navy, 1798.
b) **IRELAND: Pikeman, 1798.**
c) **FRANCE: Master Gunner,**
Navy, 1798.

The rebels of the "98' rebellion wore civilian clothes—usually 'Sunday best'—consisting of felt 'flowerpot' hat, tail-coat, corduroy breeches, stockings and shoes. However, some attempt at uniformity was made by the wearing of green ribbons and cockades, white hat-bands or (for those in authority) green bands with gold harp and the legend ERIN GO BRAGH ('Ireland For Ever') or EQUALITY LIBERTY; green feathers and handkerchiefs were also common and, if no green were available, any colour except the loyalist orange was used. A few officers wore green coats with yellow facings, the radical Bagenal Harvey having silver epaulettes on his ordinary clothes. Another leader, Roache, was seen by Charles Jackson wearing civilian dress with 'two most enormous epaulettes and a silk sash and a belt in which he carried a large pair of horse pistols', but the only proper uniform Jackson ever saw was that of a shoe-black named Monk, a United Irish captain who had a green 'helmet-cap' with white feather, green light dragoon jacket with silver lace, and green breeches with silver seam. One rebel leader in the action at Enniscorthy was seen wearing a scarlet coat which glittered in the sun (probably captured from the North Cork Militia at Oulart Hill the day before), but without boots! Though fowling-pieces and captured muskets were used, the rebels' standard weapon was the home-made pike.

French naval ratings had no 'dress regulations' as such but wore a loose, dark blue jacket with double row of brass buttons over a white shirt, usually worn with the shirt-collar outside the jacket, a black neckerchief, wide fabric girdle (containing personal possessions) or a waistcoat, with dark blue, white, grey or striped bell-bottom trousers, and a black-varnished 'round hat' of various types, like the British or with a tall crown, usually bearing a 'tricolor' cockade or bunch of ribbon. Officers had the uniform dress illustrated, dark blue with red facings and white piping, with an increasing amount of gold foliate embroidery according to rank, the lower ranks (Lieut. and Ensign) having no embroidery; army-style epaulettes were worn corresponding to the equivalent rank (i.e. Naval lieutenant = Army captain; Naval ensign = Army lieutenant, etc.). From 1798 flag officers were further distinguished by coloured sashes (red, light blue or 'tricolor') as in the army. The white waistcoat illustrated was reserved for summer, red being worn in winter. Naval gunners wore army-style blue uniforms with red facings, as illustrated, and cocked hats. Gold hat-lace was reserved for the ranks of captain and upwards.

42 FRANCE:
a) **Bonaparte, 1799.**
b) **'Inspecteur aux Revues',**
1800.
c) **Kléber, 1798.**

At the beginning of the Revolutionary War, staff uniform (particularly for generals appointed after the 'Ancien Régime') was characterized by lace-encrusted, high-collared coats, heavily-feathered hats and flamboyant 'tricolor' sashes, though epaulettes were discontinued as insufficiently egalitarian for 'Citizen-Generals'. The 1791 Regulations specified a dark blue coat with blue collar and cuffs, without turnbacks, with lace increasing with higher ranks. In 1794 scarlet collar and cuffs with white flaps were authorized, and in 1796 different ranks wore different sashes: red and white for 'général en chef', red for 'général de division' and sky-blue for 'général de brigade'. In 1798 ranks were distinguished (in addition to the amount of embroidery) as follows: 'général en chef' 'tricolor' sash, red feather panache, white plume with blue base; 'général de division' red sash, red feather panache and blue-and-white plume; 'général de brigade' sky-blue sash, blue feather panache and red-and-white plume. These regulations, however, were not always obeyed and numerous variations can be found in contemporary pictures.

Bonaparte's coat (illustrated) is taken from that worn at Marengo; the lapels could be fastened to the neck, or turned back for almost half their length to show two 'triangles'. Though 'Hessian' boots are illustrated, brown-topped riding-boots were equally common. The gold-embroidered waist-belt with plate bearing RF (République Française) supports a 'mameluke' sabre, as carried by many officers who had served in Egypt.

Kléber (from a portrait) wears his hat in a 'fore-and-aft' style, the front 'peak' sticking out to the right, an unusual appearance shown clearly in a Gros portrait. His uniform has less embroidery, and his sabre is carried on a shoulder-cord, Egyptian-style. An unusually-coloured staff uniform was that of the 'Inspecteur aux Revues', whose scarlet full dress with blue facings is taken from a contemporary picture. His uniform shows how the coat could be worn open, exposing the shirt or waistcoat.

43 FRANCE:
a) Grenadier,
Demi-Brigades de Bataille,
1798.
b) Fusilier,
Demi-Brigades de Bataille,
1798.

Plate 43 illustrates the uniform worn in Europe and at the beginning of the Egyptian campaign. The grenadier is distinguished by fur cap with 'falling' plume (upright plumes were also used; Seele in fact shows one with 'tricolor' plume—white-blue-red-white-blue-red from the top), red epaulettes, and sabres. In 1791 grenadiers' bayonet-scabbards were ordered to be carried on the cartridge-box belt like those of the fusiliers, in an attempt to standardize the 'fix-bayonets' drill which was somewhat untidy as fusiliers reached to their right and grenadiers to the combined sabre- and bayonet-frog on the left. Though the order was obeyed by some units,

the combined frog probably persisted. The grenadier's blanket-roll is secured by straps, though these were not officially authorized at the time, many using string instead of leather. The fusilier wears typical 'campaign' uniform, including linen haversack, and bayonet on the cartridge-box belt. Some units embarked for Egypt in loose trousers (the 18th, 25th, 32nd and 75th had red-and-white ticken overalls at the outset), whilst the legwear of the troops in Italy was frequently in rags. See 'Orders of Battle' for the units which comprised the Egyptian expedition.

44 FRANCE:
a) Grenadier,
9th Demi-Brigade de Bataille,
1799.
b) Chasseur,
21st Demi-Brigade Légère,
1800.

The European uniforms of the Egyptian expedition proved unsuitable for tropical service, and were soon worn out. In autumn 1798 Bonaparte introduced a new cap, 'petit casquette' or 'casquette à pouf', a peaked leather head-dress with a flap which could be lowered to shield the neck, and a pompom or worsted tuft ('pouf') in regimental colouring: 2nd Légère green, 4th Légère white/green, 21st Légère yellow/green, 22nd Légère red/green, 9th red, 13th blue, 18th black, 25th white/red, 32nd white/blue, 61st white/black, 69th white/yellow, 75th red/blue, 85th red/yellow, 88th blue/yellow. A 'tricolor' cockade was worn on the top left of the cap, and a brass grenade on each side by grenadiers, some of whom (for example those of the 25th by December 1798) also adopted all-red 'poufs'.

A single-breasted jacket was introduced, dyed with local indigo, with scarlet collar and cuffs and white turnbacks for 'Demi-Brigades de Bataille' and blue throughout for 'Légères', whose cuffs were in the traditional light infantry point. Blue shoulder-straps were worn by all fusiliers, grenadiers having red epaulettes and light infantry green. The buttons were wood, covered with cloth, brass being reserved for élite units and so scarce as to be used as currency. Legwear was varied: loose linen or cotton trousers with short gaiters, or one-piece 'gaiter-trousers' whose use was limited. Legwear was often dark blue for light infantry, but this distinction doubtless disappeared with progressive shortages of material.

Shortage of cloth caused a further change in the army's appearance, for from the end of 1799 orders of that October were enacted (the so-called 'Kléber Ordinance') by which the infantry was clothed in a similar short-tailed, single-breasted jacket, but in a myriad of colours, the whole ensemble quite dazzling when viewed *en masse*. Colour details are recorded in Appendix V, but it should be noted that many variations are recorded, in some cases the result of the interpretation of a particular shade: one viewer might describe 'crimson' as 'brown' or 'violet'; in other cases, it is likely that total standardization was never achieved, lack of sufficient cloth resulting in differences even within the same unit, and at least six demi-brigades changed the colour of their uniforms due to the unavailability of the correct material. Regimental variations were common: some grenadiers (despite the climate) apparently retained their fur caps, whilst some officers adopted unofficial trousers, those of the 9th, for example, having green breeches, or red trousers with a wide green stripe. Some sources indicate that madder-red trousers were intended for the entire army, though there is no evidence that they were ever produced; Valmont indicates them but his authority must be questionable as he also specifies coloured lapels, which were never worn on the single-breasted jacket, though they *may* have been planned initially.

The Chasseur of the 21st is minus the sabre and green epaulettes usually worn by light infantry; the unit's yellow facings were not universal due to shortage of yellow cloth, 'aurore' (orange) being substituted, and later pink. The ranks of the 21st were made up with Negro slaves, *bought* by Kléber from Abyssi-

nian slave-dealers. One universal, yet unofficial, feature carried by the French army was the water-canteen; there being no regulation issue, all manner of flasks and gourds were carried, slung over the shoulder, usually by a string.

45 FRANCE:
a) **Grenadier officer, 88th Demi-Brigade de Bataille, 1800.**
b) **Fusilier, 25th Demi-Brigade de Bataille, 1800.**
c) **Fusilier, 75th Demi-Brigade de Bataille, 1800.**

The 88th, officially dressed in crimson, actually wore violet uniforms, confirmed by a contemporary drawing and a textual reference to at least one demi-brigade in that shade. Alone amongst 'Demi-Brigades de Bataille' the 88th had pointed, light infantry cuffs, and the unusual 'bastion'-shaped collar-loop. The officer illustrated wears the ordinary bicorn, worn here 'en bataille' or across the head, instead of 'en colonne' or 'fore-and-aft'. The red falling plume was popular with grenadiers, but the Cairo town commandant, General Belliard, forbade its use in November 1800, red upright plumes or carrot-shaped tufts being worn instead. Some other ranks of certain grenadier companies retained the hat, including those of the 88th. Officers had metal buttons, not cloth-covered, grenadier officers usually having sabres, including oriental weapons.

The uniform of the 25th, officially crimson, is shown as a slightly mauvish shade. The multi-coloured appearance of the army was further enhanced by the use of 'reversed colours' for musicians, for example the 9th and 75th; others, like the 88th, dressed their musicians in the same colour as the rest but with wings (green for the 88th).

The 75th's red uniform created problems in action, both cut and colour being easily con-used with British uniforms. In March 1801 the 75th was ordered to wear shirts or greatcoats over the jacket for this reason.

6 FRANCE:
a) Chasseur,
4th Demi-Brigade Légère,
1800.
b) Fusilier,
88th Demi-Brigade de
Bataille, 1800.
c) Grenadier,
85th Demi-Brigade de
Bataille, 1800.

The white greatcoat was ordered to be manufactured in September 1798, to combat the extreme cold of the Egyptian night, but by 1800 jackets were so ragged that to preserve what remained only the greatcoat was permitted when walking-out in Cairo. Collar and cuffs were regimentally-coloured, but shoulder-straps and buttons were of white cloth.

The rear view shows standard infantry equipment, in this case with sabre and bayonet on different belts (see Plate 43). The hide knapsack contained clothes, ammunition and food (haversacks carried extra), the greatcoat tied on with string, for only in 1806 was official provision made for leather straps for this purpose. The 'sabre-briquet' had a one-piece brass hilt, and was carried by grenadiers, pioneers, drummers and N.C.O.s of grenadiers and fusiliers; in fact until an order of 27 September 1798 it was the only official weapon of N.C.O.s, who carried muskets *officially* only after that date; it was also carried by light infantry. The cartridge-box was plain for all except grenadiers, who had grenade-badges. Non-regulation impedimenta accumulated on campaign included water-flasks or gourds; the musket-lock was frequently wrapped in cloth and the muzzle plugged to exclude the sand. One unwelcome piece of equipment issued for Bonaparte's foray into Syria was a short, double-edged stake with a length of chain attached near the head, to enable a line of planted stakes to be linked together forming a continuous 'hedge' against cavalry; many were doubtless 'lost' en route, the infantryman being sufficiently loaded already with equipment, food and ammunition.

47 FRANCE:
a) **Trooper,**
Régt des Dromadaires, 1800.
b) **Trooper,**
Régt des Dromadaires, 1799.

The most exotic of the French 'Armée d'Orient' was the Camel Corps, or 'Régiment des Dromadaires'. Small units of cavalry mounted on camels may have been formed by individual generals before Bonaparte's directive of April 1799 created the regiment from personnel drawn from grenadier companies, plus Reynier's small unit and Desaix's camel-mounted infantry. Ultimately numbering some 700 men, Kléber's shortage of cavalry mounts caused more men to be drafted into the unit, which increased from two squadrons of two companies each to three squadrons, though not all the men were mounted; on 19 March 1800, for example, strength had fallen to 250 mounted and 100 dismounted. The regiment was disbanded at the end of the Egyptian expedition.

The uniform was too complex to be covered comprehensively, but two main styles are illustrated. The original plan to clothe the regiment in grey was never adopted, the first dress uniform (June/July to December 1799) being the Arab style illustrated, including plumed turban around a red skull-cap, sky-blue 'kaftan' with white hussar braid and red half-sleeves, worn over a white-braided sky-blue dolman with red cuffs, sky-blue breeches and gaiters cut to resemble boots. Officers apparently wore a white-laced, crimson-topped 'konfederatka' with this uniform. From January to October 1800 there was a new full dress (worn by the mounted figure illustrated): a cane-framed shako with white turban, white-laced red kaftan with black fur edging, the previous dolman and either white-laced sky-blue breeches or crimson 'charoual' trousers. The third full dress, after October 1800, comprised a black cane shako with cockade and red plume at the left and white cords, white-laced red kaftan and dolman as before, white-barrelled black sash and crimson 'Hessian' boots with white lace.

Service dress was plainer, consisting from June 1799 to February 1800 of turban, dolman, breeches and boots (the breeches with a white trefoil thigh-knot, concealed by the kaftan in full dress); from February to September 1800 the same with a bicorn; in September/October 1800 the new dolman (with sky-blue collar and three, instead of five, rows of buttons), white-laced red breeches, and shako minus ornaments; and after September 1800 the bicorn, single-breasted sky-blue sleeved waistcoat with leather-strapped sky-blue overalls or white trousers; with all these service uniforms a large white cloak was worn. Due to shortage of material there was probably considerable variation in uniform, items of full and service dress probably combined with non-regulation features. Trumpeters wore hussar uniform, an extant example comprising bicorn with white lace cockade-loop and red-over-white-over-blue feather, white-laced scarlet pelisse with white fur worn over a white-laced scarlet waistcoat, scarlet breeches with white trefoil thigh-knots, white-laced 'Hessian' boots and white trumpet-cords. The dismounted company had drummers.

There was probably little standardization of arms, most personnel coming from infantry units and probably having to make do with whatever cavalry weapons were available, plus some oriental weapons. The original metal-shafted lance was soon discarded, pistols and muskets comprising the main armament. Bayonets were often secured to the muzzle by string to prevent their being wrenched off in combat, a common precaution. Infantry cartridge-boxes and either cavalry belts or oriental shoulder-cords to support the sabre were also carried. It was originally planned for each dromedary to carry two men in a pannier-type saddle, but the single-man

pattern was found more practical. Parade harness is illustrated; for active service a simpler type would be used. Food and ammunition was carried upon the saddle, with pistol butt-forwards at the front.

48 FRANCE/EGYPT:
a) FRANCE: Mameluke, 1801.
b) EGYPT: Mameluke, 1799.

The Mamelukes (Turkish 'mamlūk', a slave) were the most fearsome opponents of the French in Egypt: highly-skilled cavalry with legendary proficiency in single combat, but their lack of discipline and cohesion enabled the French to defeat them with heavy loss. In action the mameluke would first fire his carbine from horseback, then his several pairs of pistols, which he would then throw down, to be retrieved by his two 'serradj' (servants), then fling his javelins (four-foot sharpened palm-branches) and finally charge with the sabre, each man fighting as an individual. The mameluke illustrated is based upon sketches by D. V. Denon, who was present in Egypt. Head-dress consisted of a coloured silk turban, which could be worn wrapped around the chin, with an ancient helmet on top, sometimes with mail neck-guard. A mail-coat was worn under the kaftan; the wide sash was universal, though all colouring at the wearer's discretion. A British officer, Lieut. Richard Caton, described the arms: 'Every Mameluke is formidably armed with a long carbine, two braces of pistols; one in his holsters; the other in his girdle, together with a stiletto and sabre, well tempered and with the keenest edge possible. He carries at his saddle bow a battle axe and his slave follows with his javelin.'

Several thousand Egyptians followed the French army home, including some who had served as irregular cavalry in the campaign. Two hundred and forty of the best were formed into a mameluke squadron in October 1801, eventually becoming the most exotic part of Napoleon's Imperial Guard, though their oriental composition dwindled as French

118

recruits were drafted in. Uniform was largely a matter of personal taste, that illustrated from a contemporary painting; note the large oriental stirrups. Officers' uniform was much richer, Hoffman showing a captain with huge white turban around a red skull-cap, both gold-encrusted, with enormous white plume; gold-laced short orange coat with half-sleeves over a gold-laced green jacket, crimson trousers, gold-striped white girdle, gold-laced sky-blue shabraque with gold tassels hung all round, and gold-embossed green leather harness, equally bedecked with gold tassels. This appearance initially led to some difficulty; for example when the celebrated Capt. Ibrahim first went to Paris he was hooted and insulted by a crowd on account of his unusual dress. His response was characteristically mameluke: he shot two of the crowd dead!

49 BRITAIN:
a) **Grenadier,**
61st Foot (Egypt), 1801.
b) **Private,**
90th (Perthshire Volunteers)
Light Infantry, 1800.

Some of the British infantry sent to Egypt may have worn West Indian tropical dress—plain jacket or sleeved waistcoat and 'gaiter-trousers' or loose overalls, though there are few contemporary pictorial records. De Loutherberg shows the infantry at Alexandria wearing shakos (see Plate 63), with officers in 'round hats', but pictures of the 61st painted by a member of the regiment show what was probably standard dress: ordinary jacket, loose trousers and 'round hat' with white band. The grenadiers are shown in the flat-topped fur cap illustrated, a style also worn by the 15th. The design of plate is not evident from the original. The man illustrated is examining a typical 'round hat', some of which are shown with plumes.

The 90th (Perthshire Volunteers) was raised in 1794 by Thomas Graham of Balgowan, a middle-aged gentleman of no military experience but with a personal grudge

against republican France following the desecration of his wife's coffin by revolutionary officials. His regiment was selected to train as light infantry to remedy the shortage of such specialist troops; it is said that Sir John Moore was influenced in his later light infantry training by watching the 90th at drill. After serving in Minorca the regiment was sent to Egypt in 1801, winning its first battle-honour at Mandora (13 March) when it repelled French cavalry. The uniform was different from that of the line, most particularly the 'Tarleton' helmet with bearskin crest, which did not extend so far as to obscure the bugle-horn badge on the front. An extant helmet (worn by Lieut. Col. Rowland Hill—later Wellington's deputy—at Mandora) has only a single chain on either side to secure the turban. This helmet reputedly had a tactical effect at Mandora, the French presuming the 90th to be dismounted cavalry and an easy 'kill', only to be driven off in disorder. The buff-leather equipment was left unwhitened to match the facings; officers' lace was gold, that of the other ranks white with blue and buff stripes. Blue-grey pantaloons were worn by the rank-and-file (buff for officers), hence the nickname 'Perthshire Greybreeks'; though an Inspection Report shortly after the campaign notes 'buff breeches and long gaiters', perhaps a re-issue replacing those worn out on campaign. On landing in Egypt, knapsacks were left aboard ship, only a haversack, canteen and rolled blanket slung on the back being used.

50 BRITAIN:
a) **Grenadier, Regt de Roll,**
1798 (full dress).
b) **Officer,**
Regt de Roll (Egypt).
c) **Private,**
Regt de Roll (Egypt).

First of the excellent Swiss corps in British service was that formed in 1794 by Baron de Roll, previously a captain in the 'Gardes Suisses'. Recruited in Switzerland, it marched through Austria and Italy, to Corsica and Elba and in 1797 joined Stuart's British force in Portugal. Stuart was unimpressed with the unit but de Roll greatly improved discipline and training before the Egyptian campaign.

The original uniform was similar to that of the 'Ancien Régime', scarlet faced sky-blue with white lace, including chevrons on the lower sleeves. The grenadier illustrated (from a contemporary picture) has epaulettes and bearskin cap. Later the jacket was worn, coloured as before, loops in pairs, and fur-crested 'round hat' with red turban and white plume tipped red. C. C. P. Lawson recorded a contemporary picture showing uniform in Egypt: an officer wears a low-crowned grey hat with wide brim, and old-style coatee with turned-down collar; the 'epaulettes' are actually fringed black shoulder-straps. A private is shown wearing a jacket, apparently without lace save for one loop on the collar, a black 'round hat' and 'gaiter-trousers'. This jacket may have been worn by other units in Egypt, perhaps a version of West Indian dress or the uniform issued to recruits. For example, C-in-C's letter, 30 July 1791, states: '... for recruits enlisted for Regiments stationed abroad, viz. 1 red jacket with sleeves, 1 pair gaiter trowsers ... 1 round hat ...'; Warrant for recruits' clothing, 16 December 1795: 'The dress shall consist of one red jacket to button all the way down, with a collar of the facing ...'; and Inspection Return, 14th Foot, 1791: 'Regiment appeared in the linen waistcoats and long trouser-breeches of the West Indies'. Loftie shows an officer of the 16th at Surinam (1804) wearing a similar, single-breasted jacket.

51 HANOVER/PRUSSIA:
a) **HANOVER: Officer, 4th Regt.**
b) **PRUSSIA: Officer, 5th Cuirassiers, Gala uniform.**
c) **PRUSSIA: Officer, Fusiliers of the Westphalian Brigade.**

Plates 51 and 52 are taken from engravings by F. von Köller, 1802, depicting uniforms of a slightly earlier date. Whilst in some cases doubtful features are included—for example a French officer in gaiter-trousers with *horizontal* red, white and blue stripes—Köller's plates are useful to compare the national distinctions of uniforms which had a similar basic design. No matter what his uniform, the nationality of an officer was identified by his cockade and sash, relics of the seventeenth-century 'field sign' needed to identify friend from foe before the advent of 'uniform' as such.

The Hanoverian uniform is obviously British in style, even to the GR cypher of the shoulder-belt plate. His national distinction is the yellow sash. Although in France the term 'fusilier' indicated an ordinary, 'centre company' private, in the Prussian and other German armies it indicated light infantry. The officer illustrated wears the green fusilier coat, though red skirt-lining is shown in the original, apparently in error, as the red lining was not introduced until 1799, the uniform illustrated pre-dating this year. The cuirassier officer wears 'Gala' uniform, worn on special parade and social occasions. The nationality of both Prussians is proclaimed by the silver-and-black sash.

52 DENMARK/PORTUGAL:
a) DENMARK: Officer, Norwegian Guard Regt.
b) PORTUGAL: Officer, Olivenca Regt.

Two further uniforms from Köller. The Danish officer wears their traditional scarlet and the red-and-gold Danish sash. The Portuguese officer probably belongs to the 1st (Olivenca) Regt, wearing the traditional blue Portuguese uniform. Of especial interest is his cross-shaped cockade, red with blue edging; most contemporary pictures of a slightly later period show the Portuguese cockade as bow-shaped or, during the later part of the Peninsular War, circular.

53 FRANCE:
a) Trooper, 11th Chasseurs à Cheval, 1801.
b) Trooper, 7th Hussars, 1800.

The Chasseurs à Cheval formed the bulk of the light cavalry. In 1791 there were twelve regiments, whose facings were: 1st–3rd scarlet, 4th–6th yellow, 7th–9th pink, 10th–12th crimson, the 2nd, 5th, 8th and 11th having green collars and the 3rd, 6th, 9th and 12th green cuffs. Three more regiments were raised in 1792, and eight more in 1793; the 17th and 18th were disbanded in 1794, their numbers remaining vacant, and one new corps, the 24th, raised. The green chasseur uniform was not unlike that of the hussars, comprising braided dolman or 'caracot', to which some officers unofficially added a pelisse. In service dress the 'surtout' (a plain, lapelled coat in the same colouring) was used increasingly, until by the early 1800s the use of the dolman was an exception. The figure illustrated (from a contemporary painting) has a popular style: the dolman worn open to reveal the braided waistcoat underneath. The head-dress was the fur-crested 'Tarleton' until replaced by the mirliton by the mid-1790s, and in 1801 the shako proper. The remainder of the uniform (breeches, weapons and horse-furniture) was hussar in style.

The hussar illustrated (from an extant uniform) shows the development from the uniforms of Plates 2 and 17. By the late 1790s the peaked mirliton had developed into a shako with a 'wing', confirmed in 1801 by the adoption of the shako proper, though the wing was retained for some time. The uniform illustrated shows a variation on the usual hussar style, the dolman worn over the (often sleeveless) waistcoat, like the chasseur, with pelisse discarded. The sabretache had a green face with yellow edging and embroidery consisting of a numeral 7 with a wreath of palm and laurel, with horizontal fasces below and, at the bottom, a scroll bearing HUSSARDS in black. Equipment was of the standard pattern, with two shoulder-belts, supporting pouch and carbine; the 1786 carbine is illustrated.

Uniform-details for the ten hussar regiments existing in 1803 are given below.

Regt	Pelisse	Dolman	Facings	Waistcoat	Breeches	Buttons & Lace
1	sky-blue	sky-blue	scarlet	scarlet	sky-blue	white
2	brown	brown	sky-blue	sky-blue	sky-blue	white
3	grey	grey	scarlet	grey	grey	white; red lace
4	scarlet	blue	scarlet	white	blue	yellow
5	white	sky-blue	white	sky-blue	sky-blue	yellow
6	blue	scarlet	scarlet	scarlet	blue	yellow
7	dark green	dark green	scarlet	scarlet	scarlet	yellow
8	dark green	dark green	scarlet	scarlet	scarlet	white
9	sky-blue	scarlet	sky-blue	sky-blue	sky-blue	yellow
10	sky-blue	sky-blue	scarlet	scarlet	sky-blue	white

For the first six regiments the collar was of the dolman-colour, and of the facing-colour for the remainder.

54 AUSTRIA:
   a) Field Marshal, 1800.
   b) Officer, Sappers, 1800.
   c) Private, Artillery, 1800.

55 AUSTRIA:
   a) Troopers, Dragoons, 1799.
   b) Trooper,
   1st Light Dragoons, 1800.

The Field Marshal illustrated (after Otten-feld) wears a uniform similar to the infantry style, but with turn-down collar. Not until 1798 did the dress regulations make a distinction between campaign and 'Gala' (parade) uniform, the green plume being worn only in full dress. The broad gold lace trimming had an interwoven zigzag band; the gold-and-black sash was worn by all officers. The decoration worn by the figure illustrated is the Order of Maria Theresa.

There were *five* separate engineer corps in the Austrian army, all with their own staff and establishment: engineers, sappers, miners, pioneers and pontooners, their duties often overlapping; the pioneers, for example, did the same work as the sappers but were independent because they came under the direction of the general staff, not the Director General of Engineers, and because they were largely Bohemian and Moravian in composition. Though the pioneers were mostly skilled craftsmen, before 1800 it was usual to recruit sappers from rejects from infantry regiments, the calibre only improving after 1801 when recruits were taken from civilian life. Engineer, sapper and miner officers wore similar uniform, of bluish-grey with red facings. Miners and sappers had black-over-yellow plumes and engineers black; other ranks' 'round hats' had upturned rear brim like the officers, but without the lace; their uniforms were grey, faced red, and arms either a pistol in a black leather holster or a musket, and a saw-bladed sabre. Austrian artillery wore brown uniforms faced red, the man illustrated after J. B. Seele. The jacket was similar in cut to that of the sapper officer illustrated, but with shorter tails.

The uniform of the Austrian medium cavalry is a complicated and unclear subject. Before 1798 there existed white-clad dragoons and green-clad 'chevaulegers', but in that year the two were amalgamated to form 'light dragoons', wearing green with coloured facings: 1st and 4th scarlet, 2nd and 14th golden-yellow, 3rd and 5th orange, 6th and 8th pink, 7th sulphur-yellow, 9th and 15th black, 10th and 12th sky-blue, 11th and 13th pompadour-red. However, the regulations regarding uniform-colour were apparently disregarded as contemporary pictures show dragoons wearing green, light dragoons in white, etc.; probably the old dragoon regiments wore their white uniform at least until they wore out, when new green or even white would be issued. However, as the light dragoons were again split into dragoons and chevaulegers in 1801, it seems unlikely that any standard uniform was adopted before the dragoons officially reverted to white in 1801 (some probably *never* having adopted the green); but three of the new chevauleger regiments also wore white, green not becoming universal for them until 1806.

In other respects the uniform was reasonably standard: white breeches and knee-boots or grey overalls and the brass-fitted classical helmet; the one Mounted Jäger regiment, 'Graf Bussy', wore a jäger-style helmet with green crest, light green uniform faced grass-green with yellow buttons. Horse-furniture for all was red, the shabraque bearing the Imperial cypher, with red valise and white sheepskin. Leather equipment was white (black for Mounted Jägers), the carbine-ramrod attached to the shoulder-belt to prevent its loss when firing from horseback. An interesting variation on dragoon uniform is shown by Seele, including a leather cap with low crest, false front and narrow peak, with large brass plate and black-over-yellow plume (in some cases covered by an oilskin tube); the drawing is dated 1799 and presumably shows campaign dress, but being in sepia the regiment cannot be identified by facing-colour. The heavy-bladed dragoon broadsword with disc hilt was the inspiration for the British 1796-pattern heavy cavalry sabre; even the Austrian sword-drill was adopted by Britain in an attempt to raise the British cavalry to the same standard of excellence as the Austrians.

56 BADEN/PRUSSIA:
a) BADEN: Officer.
Leib-Regt, full dress,
1802.
b) PRUSSIA: Officer,
Magdeburg Hussars, 1800.

Uniforms of the Baden army were styled on those of Prussia, as obvious from the figure illustrated. The dress uniform included the national silver, red and yellow sash, and a silver cord which hung from the rear of the right shoulder. In ordinary dress, a plain hat was worn, unlaced save for cockade-loop, and a blue double-breasted coat, fastened to waist-level, with red cuffs, lining, and 'stand-and-fall' collar.

The Magdeburg Hussar officer is taken from a print by Ramm. This unit was originally raised as a bodyguard for Prince Ferdinand of Brunswick in 1761, and disbanded upon the capitulation of Magdeburg in 1806. A further hussar corps raised in 1792 was the 11th or Anspach Hussar Battalion (not 'Regiment'). Until 1804 the uniform comprised a black mirliton with white lace and green cords, plumed as for the other hussar regiments, yellow dolman faced green, green pelisse with brown fur, white lace and breeches, white-barrelled green girdle, initially a red sabretache and later black leather with brass FWR cypher; green shabraque with yellow vandyke edging and white lace, and equipment like the other hussars.

57 NAPLES/CISALPINE REPUBLIC:
a) NAPLES: Private,
Regt Albania, 1800.
b) CISALPINE REPUBLIC:
Fusilier Lieutenant, 1801.

Albanian troops had long been employed by Naples, two infantry regiments and a rifle battalion taking part in the 1798 campaign against France, the riflemen distinguishing themselves covering the retreat after the defeat at Civitacastellana. The Albanians fought on against the French after the disbandment of the army following King Ferdinand's escape to Sicily, and many Albanians joined the 'Holy Faith' royalist guerrilla army of Cardinal Ruffo which continued the fight. Two Albanian regiments were raised, the Regt 'Albania' and the 'Cacciatori Albanesi' Btn (Albanian Rifles). The uniform illustrated includes a cap with busby-style ornaments and Royal cypher, a curiously-shaped tunic and 'gaiter-trousers' (white trousers without the leather reinforcing were also worn), with the Bourbon lily motif on the belt-plate.

Like many French satellites, the Cisalpine Republic based its uniform on French designs. One unusual feature can be seen on the officer's undress 'surtout' illustrated—the indication of rank by epaulette-design (as in the French army) and, unusually, by the number of buttons worn on the collar-patch: lieutenant two, captain three, etc. The red-white-green 'tricolor' cockade and plume were obviously inspired by the French version. In summer, white waistcoat and breeches were worn; the uniform illustrated is in accordance with the dress regulations of 16 October 1801. On 1 January of the following year the Cisalpine Republic changed its name to the Italian Republic.

123

58 FRANCE:
   a) Trooper, 8th Cavalry, campaign dress, 1800.
   b) N.C.O., 5th Dragoons, 1800.

In 1791 the 24 French heavy cavalry regiments all wore the bicorn, blue coat with cut-open lapels, breeches and riding-boots; facing-colours borne on collar, cuffs, cuff-flaps, lapels and turnbacks were scarlet for Regts 1 to 6, 7th–12th yellow, 13th–18th crimson and 19th–24th pink; blue collar and cuff-flaps for the 2nd, 5th, 8th, 11th, 14th, 17th, 20th and 23rd, and blue cuffs for the 3rd, 6th, 9th, 12th, 15th, 18th, 21st and 24th; regiments numbered 25 to 29 (in 1793) had orange facings, and, following the emigration of the 15th in 1793, those with higher numbers were renumbered accordingly.

The trooper illustrated is taken from a Kobell illustration, showing one regiment which wore the cuirass, the old 'Cuirassiers du Roi'; the cuirass was adopted by the remainder in 1802–03 when twelve regiments became cuirassiers, the 13th and 18th becoming dragoons and the balance disbanded. Kobell shows a variation of the regulation uniform, the 8th having a yellow collar; the blue shoulder-straps piped in the facing-colour are obscured by the cuirass. The plume, black with facing-coloured tip, is shown on a hat worn 'fore-and-aft', though 'en bataille' was as common. A new bicorn was introduced in 1801 (replaced by the cuirassier helmet in 1804), an order of that year specifying its wearing '. . . with front point in the direction of the left eye, with right eyebrow almost covered, the left uncovered by an inch . . .'. Kobell does not illustrate the sabre clearly but appears to show the barred-hilted 1786 type; he shows the half-shabraque and sheepskin edged in the facing colour; cloth holster-caps, lace-edged like the shabraque, were rarely used on campaign.

Dragoons (medium cavalry, originally mounted infantry but by this time true cavalry) totalled eighteen regiments in 1791, wearing green coats with facing-colours borne on collar, cuffs, cuff-flaps, lapels and turn-backs: 1st–6th scarlet, 7th–12th crimson, 13th–18th dark pink; green cuffs for the 3rd, 6th, 9th, 12th, 15th and 18th, and green collar and cuff-flaps for the 2nd, 5th, 8th, 11th, 14th and 17th; the 19th to 21st (raised 1793) had yellow facings. The head-dress was the classical brass helmet with large horsehair mane and fur turban (often leopardskin for officers). Plumes worn in full dress were usually black with facing-coloured tip; in ordinary dress a small pompom was borne instead. There were regimental variations, including the N.C.O. illustrated, from a Lejeune picture, showing red plume and collar, and red-edged silver rank-stripes on the sleeves; green grenades were borne on the turnbacks. The man illustrated has an unusual 'shoulder-belt'—the regulation waist-belt lengthened to go over the shoulder.

59 FRANCE:
   a) Trooper, 1st Carabiniers, campaign dress, 1800.
   b) Driver, Artillery, 1801.

The two carabinier regiments were the élite of the heavy cavalry; both wore cavalry uniform (see Plate 58) with scarlet facings, only the cuff-flaps distinguishing the 1st Regt (scarlet flaps) from the 2nd (blue). The fur cap and red epaulettes indicated 'élite' status, though the bicorn was also worn. The figure illustrated (complete with unusual service-dress overalls) is taken from Kobell, with one exception: Kobell shows the lapels closed to the waist, a style impossible with the cut-open pattern of coat then in use. It is unlikely that Kobell was portraying an unofficial variation in uniform (though it is possible) but more likely represents a slight misinterpretation. Kobell also shows white turnbacks, though red with blue grenade-badges was the regulation. The shabraque is not shown clearly by Kobell, though the sheepskin-fronted pattern was used. Dress shabraques included holster-caps of the same colouring, with grenades borne on the shabra

124

que rear-corners instead of the regimental number as in the cavalry; one contemporary picture shows the badge to have a blue ball, edged red, with red flames; similar grenade-badges or white numerals were borne on the ends of the valise. Leather equipment was buff with white edges; normally the musket or carbine was strapped to the right of the saddle, though Zix shows a carabinier with a second shoulder-belt supporting a spring-clip for carbine-suspension. The shoulder-belt supported a black cartridge-box with brass grenade badge. 1801 regulations gave clearer details about the pattern of cap, specifying a red cloth rear disc bearing a white cross, and red cords, white cords being used before this date. Sabres, carried from a frog on the waist-belt, had distinctive designs, with a semi-basket hilt bearing an embossed grenade, a device repeated on the waist-belt plate.

The artillery driver illustrated—from a contemporary picture—wears a uniform officially 'iron grey', a colour which contemporary pictures suggest had a bluish tinge. The version illustrated includes a tail-less jacket with curiously-shaped lapels, and tight breeches.

60 FRANCE:
   a) Trumpeter,
   Horse Grenadiers,
   Consular Guard, c.1801.
   b) Drummer, Grenadiers,
   Consular Guard, c.1801.

Like every European nation whose sovereign had a bodyguard corps, even Republican France had its 'guard' troops. Though the King's 'Gardes françaises' was disbanded, various short-lived corps were created: the 'Gardes Constitutionelle du Roi' (September 1791–May 1792), the 'Gardes de l'Assemblée Nationale'; the 'Garde de la Convention' which became the 'Garde du Corps Législatif' in 1795, the 'Garde du Directoire' and finally the 'Garde Consulaire', the two latter being the forerunners of Napoleon's legendary Imperial Guard.

The uniform of these corps was styled like that of the regular army, whether infantry, cavalry, etc. and by the period illustrated had virtually evolved into the famous costume of Napoleon's Guard. Two variations illustrated both belong to musicians, who traditionally wore most elaborate uniform, both of the consular Guard ('Gardes des Consuls' or 'Garde Consulaire'). The 'Grenadiers à Cheval' originated in the 'Garde du Directoire', wearing a dark blue uniform faced scarlet, similar to infantry grenadiers and line carabiniers, with bearskin cap. The trumpeters wore richly-laced uniform with sumptuous horse-furniture and ornate bicorn, the illustration, after Hoffman, including sky-blue trumpet-banner with intersecting gold lines and a bursting-grenade badge in the centre, and a sabre with ornate shell-guard. The 'Grenadiers à Pied' also originated in the 'Garde du Directoire'; the drummer illustrated (after Hoffman) wears ordinary uniform, with the addition of orange musicians' lace and epaulettes atop the musicians' wings. The drum-shell is quite plain, only the hoops being decorated. Both horse and foot grenadiers had bursting-grenade turnback-badges.

In 1800, four years before the title changed to 'Imperial Guard', the Consular Guard had the very moderate strength (compared to the massive Imperial Guard of later years) of two battalions of grenadiers, one of chasseurs, three squadrons of horse grenadiers and one of chasseurs à cheval, and a company of horse artillery: a grand total of only 3,657 men including staff.

61 FRANCE:
   a) Carabinier,
   14th Demi-Brigade Légère,
   1800.
   b) Musician,
   14th Demi-Brigade Légère,
   1800.
   c) Chasseur,
   Light Infantry, 1801.

The dark green light infantry uniform of the 'Ancien Régime' persisted in the 1791 regulations, the infantry-style coat having facing-colours on collar, cuffs, and cuff-flaps: 1st–3rd Regts scarlet, 4th–6th yellow, 7th–9th pink, 10th–12th crimson; green collar and cuff-flaps for 2nd, 5th, 8th, and 11th; green cuffs for 3rd, 6th, 9th and 12th. The 13th and 14th (formed 1792) had white facings, the 14th green collar and cuff-flaps. In light infantry units 'chasseurs' and 'carabiniers' were equivalent to fusiliers and grenadiers of the line; head-dress was the fur-crested helmet (though carabiniers also wore fur caps without plates), and bicorns. In 1793 short-tailed blue coats were adopted, with the pointed-ended lapels which remained a light infantry distinction throughout the Napoleonic Wars. Facing-colours disappeared, though collar and cuff-flaps were usually red, the piping white, waistcoat and breeches dark blue and the bicorn was adopted in place of the helmet. Numerous regimental variations included epaulettes for all companies (green with red crescents, or plain green, for chasseurs), long-tailed coats for officers, blue or scarlet pointed cuffs, fur caps, mirlitons or shakos.

In 1801 the shako proper was introduced, with hunting-horn badge, green cords, and plume often borne at the left, coloured green, green-and-yellow, green-and-red, green-and-sky-blue, or red for carabiniers. The chasseur illustrated (from a contemporary painting) wears regulation dress plus green epaulettes, and a shako with rosette instead of badge, and plume at the front. Illustrations by the same contemporary artist show a carabinier with a red upper band on the shako, red plume and cords, epaulettes and breeches-stripe; short gaiters were usual, edged red for carabiniers. Sabres were carried by many chasseurs as well as carabiniers, whose sword-knots were red.

A more exotic variation was worn by the 14th: long-tailed coats with red-flapped cuffs bearing four buttons, and the mirliton; carabiniers had red mirliton-wing and plume, epaulettes and gaiter-edging; chasseurs green plume with red tip, sky-blue wing with sky-blue or white tassel, green epaulettes with red

crescents and green gaiter-lace; and the voltigeur (skirmisher) company, when added in 1804, green plume with yellow tip, yellow wing, yellow collar piped red, green epaulettes with yellow crescents and green gaiter-lace; officers' lace was silver. Although the drummers' only distinction was a 'tricolor' plume, musicians wore the green-and-crimson uniform illustrated.

62 FRANCE/BRITAIN:
a) FRANCE: Infantryman, San Domingo, 1802.
b) FRANCE: 'Chef de Musique', San Domingo, 1802.
c) BRITAIN: Cuban Chasseur, 1796.

Although actions in the West Indies were not part of the Revolutionary Wars proper, they swallowed thousands of troops who might otherwise have been employed in Europe, casualties from sickness being many times greater than those from action. The 'Chef de Musique' (bandmaster) of the San Domingo garrison (after 'Job') wears an elaborate musicians' uniform, including baggy 'mameluke' trousers, wide sash and oriental sabre, all suggesting service in Egypt. The infantryman's uniform has only one concession to tropical service, the wide-brimmed 'round hat' turned up at the front.

The Cuban Chasseur illustrated represents the irregular units employed in the West Indies. During the Jamaican Maroon revolt, Britain enrolled some forty Spanish irregulars, each with three dogs, to act as trackers and police, receiving (besides pay) a bounty of 960 dollars for every rebel apprehended. The very appearance of these men was sufficient to suppress the revolt faster than military force could have accomplished. Their 'uniform' and equipment was described as '. . . a check shirt open at the collar to expose the neck from which hangs a crucifix, a wide pair of check trousers, a straw hat or rather one manufactured of morras thatch, divided into small filaments, 7 or 8 inches in the rim with shallow round crown ... a pair of untanned leather shoes ... a long straight machet, longer than a dragoon sword and twice as thick, sharpened at the end ... the point not unlike the old Roman sword. The handle is without a guard but scalloped to admit the fingers'. Their dogs, 'the size of a very large hound with ears erect' were secured by a cotton rope attaching muzzle, collar and the chasseur's belt, so that muzzle and collar could be slipped in one motion when pursuing a fugitive. So savage were the animals that they chased the British General Walpole into his carriage when he requested a demonstration of their capabilities!

63 BRITAIN:
   a) Private,
   Battalion Company,
   20th Foot, 1800–01.
   b) Officer, Light Company,
   34th Foot, c.1800.

In the late 1790s British infantry uniform took on Austrian style. In early 1796 the coat was ordered to be made with 'lappels (sic) ... as at present; down to the waist; but to be made so, as either to button over occasionally; or to clasp close with hooks and eyes, all the way down to the bottom', with the standing collar officially authorized. Perhaps this order was never implemented, for the short-tailed, single-breasted Austrian-style jacket was authorized in 1797, originally with turnbacks starting below the lowest breast-button, later receding to a position on the side of the hips. Officers' uniforms continued to be double-breasted, the top of the lapels sometimes folded back to form two facing-coloured triangles. Collar, cuffs and shoulder-straps were facing-coloured, red wings for 'flank' companies, all shoulder-ornaments usually having worsted edging. Regimentally-coloured lace was retained, white for sergeants. The colour of the other ranks' uniform was a dull red (sometimes described ambiguously as 'brick red'); possibly

sergeants' uniforms were scarlet like those of the officers.

The bicorn increased in size, an order of 22 September 1796 specifying white plume and small tassels at the corners of mixed white and facing-colour (crimson and gold for officers), with white hat-lace discontinued. This hat is shown held by the private illustrated, who wears the 'stovepipe' shako authorized in 1799 and first produced in 1800. The leather cap had a large brass front-plate often bearing the regimental number in addition to the usual heraldic devices, with white plume for grenadiers, white-over-red for battalion companies and green for light companies, though the 'round hat' was retained by some of the latter, as were fur grenadier caps for full dress. The private of the 20th illustrated has a shako-plate incorporating the number xx, and lace with red and blue lines at the edges of each loop.

Regimental variations included diverse light company head-dress: laced shakos, 'Tarleton' helmets or, as illustrated, a leather cap with white fur (or feather?) transverse crest. This uniform (after William Loftie) shows the officers' version of the new coat. A similar cap, less pointed, was worn by the 31st and (earlier) by the 7th. Blue breeches were quite common for officers: the 16th, for example, had them with black knots on the thighs, and the 43rd with mixed red-and-silver knots (though some of these may have been the result of individual whim). The officers of some units, for example the 16th, unofficially adopted additional lace on the breast of their coats.

64 HELVETIAN REPUBLIC/SAXONY:
   a) HELVETIAN REPUBLIC:
   Chasseur,
   Helvetian Legion, 1802.
   b) SAXONY: Hussar, 1803.

Plate 64 illustrates two examples of the classic light cavalry uniform. The Helvetian (or Helvetic) Republic had a regular army called 'The Legion' and a militia named 'Élite'. The

Chasseurs à Cheval of the Legion wore French-style chasseur uniform with mirliton, in the Helvetian 'tricolor' of red, green and yellow. In 1804 the unit was incorporated in the French 19th Chasseurs. The Infantry of the Legion had green uniforms with black collar, cuffs and lapels and wore the 'Corsican hat'—a 'round hat' with upturned brim—with yellow grenadier epaulettes.

The Saxon hussar (from a Holtzmann engraving of 1803) wears typical hussar uniform, worn by Saxony's only hussar unit (raised 1791) until a sky-blue uniform with shako was introduced in 1810.

FRANCE/PRUSSIA

A a) France: Chasseur, Paris National Guard, 1790.
  b) Prussia: Musketeer, Infantry, 1790.

BAVARIA/PRUSSIA/AUSTRIA

B (left to right, top to bottom):
a) Bavaria: 'Rumford Kaskett'.
b) Prussia: Officer's cap, Grenadiers, 1798–99.
c) Prussia: N.C.O.'s cap, Regt Herzog Karl Wilhelm Ferdinand v. Braunschweig (21st), 1785.
d) Austria: Hussar shako, c.1799.
e) Prussia: Musketeer's 'Kaskett'.

FRANCE

C a) Flag, District de St Jacques-du-Haut-Pas, Paris National Guard, 1789.
  b) Flag, District de St Louis-en-Lisle, Paris National Guard, 1789.

131

FRANCE

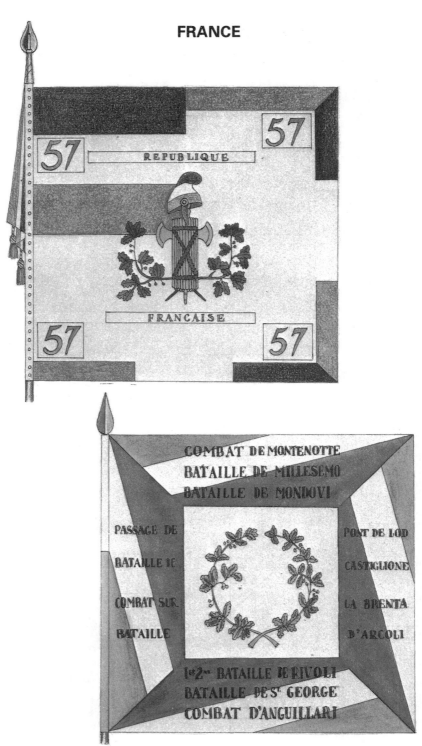

D a) Flag, 2nd Btn, 57th Demi-Brigade, 1794.
  b) Flag, 19th Demi-Brigade, 1797.

FRANCE/RUSSIA

a) France: Standard, 1st Carabiniers, 1791–94.
b) Russia: Infantry flag, Armée de Condé.

F a) Sardinia: Sergeant, Regt 'Lombardia', 1792.
   b) Papal States: Fusilier, Battn 'Castel S. Angelo', 1794.

Black and White Plate Descriptions

A FRANCE/PRUSSIA
a) FRANCE: Chasseur,
Paris National Guard, 1790.
b) PRUSSIA: Musketeer,
Infantry, 1790.

The Paris National Guard chasseur uniform is described in the text to Plate 4; green epaulettes and sword-knot, red-laced gaiters, dark blue waistcoat, breeches and girdle with red lace, green or green-over-white plume. Pistols were tucked behind, or hooked on to, girdle.

The Prussian infantry uniform is described in the text to Plate 5, including dark blue coat (see Appendix VI for facing-colours), with or without lace loops, and the 'kaskett' cap, the high front and rear flaps of which could be let down.

B BAVARIA/PRUSSIA/AUSTRIA
a) BAVARIA:
'Rumford Kaskett'.
b) PRUSSIA: Officer's cap,
Grenadiers, 1798–99.
c) PRUSSIA: N.C.O.'s cap,
Regt Herzog Karl Wilhelm
Ferdinand v. Braunschweig
(21st), 1785.
d) AUSTRIA: Hussar shako,
c.1799.
e) PRUSSIA:
Musketeer's 'Kaskett'.

The 'Rumford Kaskett' illustrated (see Plates 13–14) is taken from an extant example; note absence of chinscales, and the distinctive white mane of the grenadiers.

The two Prussian grenadier caps illustrate the change in style. The N.C.O.s cap has the old brass front-plate, a straw-yellow rear and

scarlet head-band, and distinctive black-and-white N.C.O. pompom; ordinary grenadiers had pompoms with red-black-white-red segments. The 1798–99 cap (see text to Plate 5) was a curious leather cap like the old Austrian 'Kaskett', with tall leather false-front bearing brass plates, the lower bearing a black-enamelled eagle, with a black woollen edging around the top of the cap.

The musketeer's 'Kaskett' illustrated has white tape binding and white lace FWR cypher; the Austrian hussar shako, also taken from an extant item, illustrates the peakless type of cap with large yellow-and-black national cockade/pompom; a peak was added around the turn of the century.

C FRANCE:
a) Flag, District de
St Jacques-du-Haut-Pas,
Paris National Guard, 1789.
b) Flag, District de
St Louis-en-Lisle,
Paris National Guard, 1789.

These are two further examples of elaborate National Guard flags (see Plate 4). That of the District de St Jacques-du-Haut-Pas (1st Division, 1st Btn) was blue (either 'royal' or lighter) with large white cross; gold fleurs-de-lys on the blue. Central device represented the Bastille in brown, on a green base with grey smoke above; on the arms, silver Phrygian caps and gold cypher, with sky-blue scroll bearing in gold: EX SERVITUTE LIBERTAS. The reverse was the same excepting the central device, a gold crown on a disc of golden rays; gilt spear-head, white streamers with gold fringe, gold cords and tassels.

The flag of the District de St Louis-en-Lisle

(1st Div., 5th Btn) consisted of a white diamond with alternate red and blue triangles, bearing gold crosses; central device a gold ship on green sea, sky-blue scroll bearing ST. LOUIS EN LISLE in gold, gold fleurs-de-lys, and a lower gold inscription: DONNÉ PAR LES CITOYENNES DU DISTRICT. The reverse was the same excepting central device: green palm and olive branches, gold sword with silver Phrygian cap on the point, a silver spade and shepherd's crook crossed at the back, red lower scroll and sky-blue upper one reading VIS UNITA MAJOR NUNC ET SEMPER in gold. Ornamental gilt pike-head, with streamers as before.

D FRANCE:
a) Flag, 2nd Btn,
57th Demi-Brigade, 1794.
b) Flag,
19th Demi-Brigade, 1797.

Among many patterns of flag (see Plate 30) was the 1794 style of the 2nd (Centre) Btn of the 57th: white with 'tricolor' canton in the upper corner nearest the pole, blue-over-white-over-red, with 'tricolor' border; central device a bundle of lictors' rods in brown with silver axe-heads and green foliate binding, below 'tricolored' Phrygian cap (blue-over-white-over-red) with gold chinscales and bosses, with a green wreath around; all lettering gold. The 1st and 3rd Btns had flags with the 1st and 4th quarters blue and 2nd and 3rd red.

The 19th Demi-Brigade flag shows the attempt at standardization made in 1797, as issued to the Army of Italy: white central square bearing green foliate circle, with an inner four-pointed dark blue shape, red triangles along the edges and white segments between. Battle-honours were painted in gold. Reverse was the same, with the device on the central square resembling that on the 57th's flag, with all-red bonnet and no battle-honours, only the gold inscription REPUBLIQUE FRANÇAISE above the white square and DISCIPLINE ET SOUMISSION AUX LOIS MILITAIRES below. In the upper corner nearest the pole and in the corner opposite were the large gold letters DB, and in the remaining corners 19. Some flags also bore battalion-identification.

E FRANCE/RUSSIA:
a) FRANCE: Standard,
1st Carabiniers, 1791–94.
b) RUSSIA: Infantry flag,
Armée de Condé.

Cavalry standards were much smaller than infantry Colours, around 50–60 cm square. The French 1st Carabiniers flag was crimson damask (with interwoven floral design), bearing embroidered edge-decoration of gold semi-circles and silver foliage, with gold-flamed silver grenades. Central devices were gold-embroidered, save for the three silver feathers and two scrolls, the latter edged gold with red 'reverse' (where the scroll appears to fold back) and black letters: TOUJOURS AU CHEMIN DE L'HONNEUR and CARABINIERS. One gold fleur-de-lys at the bottom: the fleurs-de-lys on the other angles were obscured by 'tricolor' patches, in accordance with an order of November 1792 which instructed all monarchist symbols to be covered by 'tricolor' diamonds or squares. Reverse side was the same except the inscription on the upper scroll, which read: DISCIPLINE OBEISSANCE A LA LOI. Gilt pike-head, pole painted in red, white and blue spirals.

The colouring of the Armée de Condé flags is given in the text to Plate 29. Ordinary Russian infantry flags followed similar designs (minus cross and fleurs-de-lys), the 1797 pattern having a large central disc and contrastingly-coloured field and 'rays' (or 'corners'). The 1800 pattern changed the design of the eagle and surrounded the central device with a wreath, with a large crown above (see *Uniforms of the Retreat from Moscow*, Plate E), with the Imperial cypher within a wreath with a crown above in each corner. These flags were coloured according to the regiment's 'Inspection':

136

	Corners of 'White' (i.e. Colonel's) flag	'Coloured' flag Field	Corners	Embroidery
Brest, Lithuania, Livonia, Smolensk	black/red	black	red	silver
Dniester, Caucasus, Ukraine, Crimea	yellow/white	yellow/white	white	gold
Moscow, St Petersburg	light crimson/white	light crimson/white	white	gold
Orenburg, Siberia	yellow/green	green	yellow	gold
Finland	black/blue	blue	black	gold

(The flags illustrated in the previous three plates are shown because they illustrate patterns peculiar to the Revolutionary Wars; for the more common types and further examples, see another Blandford Colour Series title, *Military Flags of the World* (1618–1900).)

F SARDINIA/PAPAL STATES
a) SARDINIA: Sergeant, Regt 'Lombardia', 1792.
b) PAPAL STATES: Fusilier, Btn 'Castel S. Angelo'. 1794.

These are uniforms of two Italian regiments, one exhibiting Austrian influence. Regt 'Lombardia': black hat with gold lace, light blue cockade with gold loop. Light blue coat with scarlet collar and cuffs, yellow lapels, lining and turnbacks. Gold lace and gilt buttons; dark blue heart-shaped badges on turnbacks. White waistcoat and breeches, black gaiters. White belts, brass-fitted sabre.

Btn 'Castel S. Angelo': black leather helmet with brass badge and crest-edging, red cockade with yellow edge. White coat with light green collar, cuffs, turnbacks and shoulder-straps, white metal buttons; white breeches and gaiters with white metal buttons; white belts with brass plate, brown bayonet-scabbard with brass tip.

Appendix I

Uniform of French infantry, 1786 (not including 'foreign' regiments)
(x = facing-coloured distinction; otherwise lapels, cuffs, etc. were white.)

Regt

(a)	(b)	(c)	(d)	(e)	(f)	(g)	(h)	(i)	(j)	(k)	(l)	Lapels	Cuffs	Turn-backs	Buttons
1	8	14	20	28	49	41	52	70	82	30	45	x	x		Yellow
3	9	15	21	29	36	43	53	71	83	44	35	x			Yellow
4	10	16	22	31	37	47	58	73	85				x		Yellow
5	11	17	25	32	38	48	59	74	86	55	81	x	x		White
6	12	18	26	33	39	50	60	75	87	61	84	x			White
7	13	19	27	34	40	51	62	77	94	76	93		x		White
										23	42	x	x	x	Yellow
										24		x	x	x	Yellow
										46	78	x	x	x	White
										56			x		Yellow
										57				x	Yellow
										96				x	White

(a) Sky blue	(b) Black	(c) Violet	(d) Iron grey
(e) Pink	(f) Yellow	(g) Crimson	(h) Silver grey
(i) Orange	(j) Dark green	(k) Dark blue	(l) Scarlet

Appendix II

Uniform of French infantry, 1791
(x = item of facing-colour.)

Regt (a)	(b)	(c)	(d)	(e)	(f)	(g)	Lapels	Cuff-flaps and Collar	Cuffs	Buttons
1,7	13,19	25,31	37,43	49,56	67,74	82,102	x	x	x	Yellow
2,8	14,20	26,32	38,44	50,57	68,75	83	x		x	Yellow
3,9	15,21	27,33	39,45	51,58	70,78	84	x	x		Yellow
4,10	16,22	28,34	40,46	52,59	71,79	90	x	x	x	White
5,11	17,23	29,35	41,47	54,60	72,80	91	x		x	White
6,12	18,24	30,36	42,48	55,61	73,81	93	x	x		White

(a) Black (b) Violet (c) Pink (d) Sky blue
(e) Crimson (f) Scarlet (g) Dark blue

(The first of each pair of regiments had horizontal pockets, the second vertical.)

Appendix III

Uniform of French infantry, 1792
(Uniform of Regts 1 to 48 remained as Appendix II.)
(x = item of facing-colour.)

Regt (a)	(b)	(c)	(d)	(e)	Lapels	Cuff-flaps and Collar	Cuffs	Buttons
49,55	61,72	79,87	93,102	108	x	x	x	Yellow
50,56	62,73	80,88	94,103	109	x		x	Yellow
51,57	67,74	81,89	96,104	110	x	x		Yellow
52,58	68,75	82,90	98,105	111	x	x	x	White
53,59	70,77	83,91	99,106		x		x	White
54,60	71,78	84,92	101,107		x	x		White

(a) Crimson   (b) Scarlet   (c) Dark blue   (d) Dark green
(e) light green

(First of each pair of regiments had horizontal pockets, the second vertical.)

Appendix IV

Uniform of French hussars, 1795

Regt	Pelisse	Dolman	Dolman-collar	Dolman-cuffs	Lace and buttons	Breeches	Mirliton-wing	Shabraque-edging
1	sky-blue	sky-blue	sky-blue	red	white	sky-blue	scarlet/white	sky-blue
2	brown	brown	brown	red	white	sky-blue	sky-blue/black	brown
3	grey	grey	grey	red	red*	grey	white/black	red
4	scarlet	blue	blue	scarlet	yellow	blue	scarlet/black	scarlet
5	white	sky-blue	sky-blue	red	yellow	sky-blue	sky-blue/black	sky-blue
6	white	scarlet	scarlet	scarlet	yellow	blue	scarlet/black	scarlet
7	dk green	dk green	scarlet	scarlet	yellow	scarlet	scarlet/yellow	scarlet
7 bis	blue	scarlet	blue	blue	yellow	blue	scarlet/black	blue
8	dk green	dk green	scarlet	scarlet	white	scarlet	scarlet/black	scarlet
9	sky-blue	scarlet	sky-blue	sky-blue	yellow	sky-blue	sky-blue/black	scarlet
10	sky-blue	sky-blue	scarlet	scarlet	white	sky-blue	scarlet/white	scarlet
11	lt green	lt green	grey	grey	white	grey	grey/black	grey
12	sky-blue	brown	sky-blue	sky-blue	white	sky-blue	sky-blue/white	sky-blue
13	scarlet	sky-blue	scarlet	scarlet	yellow	sky-blue	scarlet/black	red

* white buttons for 3rd.

Note: First colour listed for 'mirliton-wing' indicates ground-colour, second colour of edging. Pelisse-fur grey for 7th, black for remainder.

Appendix V

French uniforms in Egypt, 1799–1801
('(Alt)' indicates alternative colour-scheme given by some sources.)

Demi-Bde		Coat	Collar/piping	Cuffs	Turnbacks	Piping
2nd Légère		lt green	dark blue/white	dark blue	dark blue	white
4th Légère		lt green	crimson/white	crimson	crimson	white
21st Légère		sky-blue	yellow/white	yellow	yellow	white
22nd Légère		sky-blue	crimson/white	crimson	crimson	white
9th		scarlet	blue/red	white	white	blue
	(Alt)	scarlet	green/white	green	green	white
13th		crimson	dark blue/white	puce	puce	white
18th		scarlet	brown	yellow	yellow	blue
	(Alt)	scarlet	yellow/blue	yellow	yellow	white
	(Alt)	brown	scarlet/blue	blue	blue	blue
25th		crimson	sky-blue/white	sky-blue	sky-blue	white
32nd		brown	scarlet/blue	orange	orange	white
	(Alt)	crimson	blue	blue	blue	blue
61st		crimson	dark blue/yellow	dark blue	dark blue	yellow
	(Alt)	crimson	blue	lt green	lt green	white
	(Alt)	brown	yellow	yellow	yellow	yellow
	(Alt)	brown	yellow/blue	lt green	lt green	blue
69th		brown	scarlet/blue	white	white	white
	(Alt)	brown	scarlet/white	scarlet	scarlet	white
75th		scarlet	sky-blue/white	sky-blue	sky-blue	white
85th		brown	scarlet/blue	yellow	yellow	white
88th		crimson	blue/white	green	green	white
	(Alt)	violet	blue/white	green	green	white
Foot Artillery		blue	red	red	red	red
Arty Artisans		blue	yellow	yellow	yellow	yellow
Miners		blue	black	black	blue	red
Balloonists		blue	green	red	blue	red
Engineers		blue	red	green	green	white

Other alternative colourings not listed above:
4th Légère: brown collar, cuffs, turnbacks.
21st Légère: red turnbacks.
13th: green piping.
18th: scarlet collar and cuffs, white turnbacks and piping.
25th: facings 'blue' (i.e. not 'sky'-blue).
69th, 75th and 85th: blue piping.
32nd and 61st: violet coats.

Appendix VI

Facing-colours of Prussian infantry regiments

Facings	White buttons: Regts	Yellow buttons: Regts
Crimson	1, 15	3, 22, 24, 27, 34, 41, 48
Pink	14	2, 12, 16
Saffron		4, 19
White	13, 39, 49	5, 17, 33, 36
Red	52	6, 8, 9, 20, 21, 25, 38
Lilac	7, 18, 23, 40, 50	
Yellow	10, 28, 55	30, 32, 44, 54
Dark grey	29	11, 37
Orange		26
Olive		31, 35
Ochre		42, 45, 47
Gold		43
Black		46
Light green	51, 53	

Lace
White: Regts 1, 4, 9, 10, 11, 12, 13, 18, 23, 45, 49: with yellow tassels, 48
Red with white tassels: 2, 17, 44
Black and white: 3
Orange with white tassels: 5
Gold: 6
Silver: 15
White and orange: 19, 22
White and red: 14, 16, 21, 24, 29
White and blue: 8, 25
Yellow: 26, 41; with white tassels, 30

Order of Battle: French Expedition to Egypt

Disembarkation, 1798

Division Desaix: 21st Légère, 61st and 88th Demi-Brigades.
Division Reynier: 9th and 85th Demi-Brigades, Légion Malte.
Division Kléber: 2nd Légère, 25th and 75th Demi-Brigades.
Division Menou: 22nd Légère, 13th and 69th Demi-Brigades.
Division Bon: 4th Légère, 18th and 32nd Demi-Brigades.
Headquarters: Guides à Cheval, Guides à Pied, Foot Artillery, Engineers, Miners, 'Ouvriers' (labour-corps), Légion Nautique.
Division Dumas: '7ème bis' Hussars, 22nd Chasseurs à Cheval, 3rd, 14th, 15th, 18th and 20th Dragoons.

Corfu Garrison

Division Chabot: 6th and 97th Demi-Brigades; detachments of Guides à Cheval and Guides à Pied.

Malta Garrison

7th and 19th Demi-Brigades; detachments 6th, 41st and 80th Demi-Brigades; one company 6th Artillery, regimental artillery companies from 4th, 19th, 30th and 69th Demi-Brigades. Small detachments from 23rd Légère, 2nd, 21st, 25th and 75th Demi-Brigades; detachment of Maltese.

Independent Units (Egypt)

Légion Grecque, Légion Cophte (Greek and Coptic Legions, raised in Egypt); two companies 'Cavalerie Syrienne'; companies, later regiment, of Mamelukes; one company 'Moghrebins' (Maghrebians); one company Egyptian artificers (formed of prisoners from Jaffa); companies of 'janissaries'—formed for police and security duty, 'Omar's' or 'Native Guides' and Barthelemy's 'Turkish Guard' in Cairo.

Bibliography

The following bibliography, which is in no way comprehensive, is divided into Section I, of works concerned principally with history (and memoirs), and Section II, concerning uniforms, though the two frequently overlap. Some of the titles listed have only a peripheral reference to the Revolutionary Wars, but are included if they provided a reference mentioned in the text; wherever possible, details of English-language editions are given. A comprehensive listing of works relative to the Napoleonic era in general is *Napoleonic Military History: A Bibliography*, ed. D.D. Horward, London 1986.

SECTION I

Alison, Sir Archibald *A History of Europe from the Commencement of the French Revolution to the Restoration of the Bourbons*, Edinburgh 1860.

Anon. *An Epitome of Military Events*, London 1800–2.

Baines, E. *History of the Wars of the French Revolution*, London 1817.

Barthorp, M.J. *Napoleon's Egyptian Campaigns 1798–1801*, London 1978.

Berry, R.P. *History of the Volunteer Infantry*, London & Huddersfield 1903.

Bryant, Sir Arthur *The Years of Endurance*, London 1942.

Bunbury, Sir Henry *Narratives of Some Passages in the Great War with France 1799–1810*, London 1854; reprinted with introduction by Hon. Sir John Fortescue, London 1927.

Carlyle, T. *History of the French Revolution*, London 1837.

Chandler, D.G. *The Campaigns of Napoleon*, London 1967.

— *Dictionary of the Napoleonic Wars*, London 1979.

Coignet, J.-R. *The Note-Books of Captain Coignet*, intro. by Hon. Sir John Fortescue, London 1928.

Cust, Hon. Sir Edward *Annals of the Wars of the Nineteenth Century*, London 1862, Vol. I (1800–06).

— *Annals of the Wars of the Eighteenth Century*, London1862; succeeding volumes to the above, Vol. IV (1783–95), V (1796–99).

Denon, D.V. *Travels in Upper and Lower Egypt during the Campaigns of Bonaparte in 1798 and 1799*, London 1803.

Dupuy, R.E., & Dupuy, T.N. *Encyclopedia of Military History*, London 1970.

Elers, G. *Memoirs of George Elers*, ed. Lord Monson & G. Levenson Gower, London 1903.

Esposito, Brig.Gen. V.J., & Elting, Col. J.R. *A Military History and Atlas of the Napoleonic Wars*, London 1964.

Fortescue, Hon. Sir John *History of the British Army*, Vol. IV, London 1906.

François, C. *From Valmy to Waterloo*, ed. R.B. Douglas, London 1906.

Glover, M. *The Napoleonic Wars: An Illustrated History 1792–1815*, London 1979

— *Warfare in the Age of Bonaparte*, London 1980.

Glover, R. *Peninsular Preparation: the Reform of the British Army 1795–1809*, Cambridge 1963.

Goodspeed, D.J. *Bayonets at St. Cloud: the Story of the 18th Brumaire,* London 1965.

Hart, Col. C.J. *History of the 1st Volunteer Battn., The Royal Warwickshire Regiment,* Birmingham 1906.

Haythornthwaite, P.J. *Napoleon's Campaigns in Italy,* London 1993.

— *The Armies of Wellington,* London 1994.

— *The Napoleonic Source Book,* London 1990.

Heriot, A. *The French in Italy 1796–99,* London 1957.

Herold, J.C. *Bonaparte in Egypt,* London 1963.

Jackson, C. *A Narrative of the Sufferings and Escape of Charles Jackson, late Resident of Wexford in Ireland, including an account by way of a Journal of several barbarous atrocities committed in June 1798 by the Irish rebels,* 1798.

James, W. *The Naval History of Great Britain from the Declaration of war by the French Republic in 1793 to the Accession of George IV,* London 1837.

Jonnès, M. de *Adventures in the Revolution and under the Consulate,* London 1929 (reprinted with introduction by M. Glover, London 1969).

Lachouque, H., & Brown, A.S.K. *The Anatomy of Glory,* London 1962.

Lloyd, C. *St. Vincent and Camperdown,* London 1963.

Marbot, J.B.A.M. *Memoirs of Baron de Marbot,* trans. A.J. Butler, London 1913.

Mignet, F.A. *History of the French Revolution,* London 1902.

Muir, Sir W. *The Mameluke or Slave Dynasty of Egypt,* London 1896.

Pakenham, T. *The Year of Liberty: the Great Irish Rebellion of 1798,* London 1969.

Phipps, Col. R.W. *The Armies of the First French Republic,* Oxford 1935–9.

Pope, D. *The Great Gamble: Nelson at Copenhagen,* London 1972.

Postgate, R. *1798: Sotry of a Year,* London 1969.

Rodger, A.B. *The War of the Second Coalition 1798–1801,* ed. C. Duffy, Oxford 1964.

Rogers, Col. H.C.B. *Napoleon's Army,* London 1974.

Ross, M. *Banners of the King: the War of the Vendée,* London 1975.

Rothenberg, G.E. *Napoleon's Great Adversaries: the Archduke Charles and the Austrian Army 1792–1814,* London 1982.

— *The Art of War in the Age of Napoleon,* London 1977.

Surtees, W. *Twenty-Five Years in the Rifle Brigade,* London 1833.

Theirs, A. *History of the French Revolution 1789–1800,* London 1895.

Tranié, J., & Carmigniani, J.-C. *Bonaparte: la Campagne d'Egypte,* Paris 1988.

— *La Patrie en Danger: Les Campagnes de la Révolution,* Paris 1987.

Vallière, Capt. de *Honneur et Fidelité: Histoire des Suisses au Service Etranger,* Neuchâtel, n.d.

Walsh, T. *Journal of the late Campaign in Egypt,* London 1803.

Warner, O. *The Glorious First of June,* London 1961.

Wilson, Sir Robert *History of the British Expedition to Egypt,* London 1803.

SECTION II

Annis, P.G.W. *Naval Swords,* London 1970.

Brandani, M., Crociani, P., & Fiorentino, M. *Uniformi Militari Italiane del Settecento,* Rome 1976.

Barthorp, M.J. *British Cavalry Uniforms,* Poole 1984.

— *British Infantry Uniforms,* Poole 1982.

Brosse, J., & Lachouque, H. *Uniformes et Costumes du Premier Empire,* Paris 1972.

Brunon, R. & J. *Bonaparte et Son Armée Après Marengo,* Salon-de-Provence, n.d.

— *Hussards*, Marseilles n.d. (reproductions of Barbier paintings).

Bucquoy, E.L. *Les Uniformes du Premier Empire* (ed. Lt.Col.Bucquoy & G.Devautour); series of books including the following, all published in Paris: *Dragons et Guides*, 1980; *La Cavalerie Légère*, 1980; *La Garde Impériale: Troupes à Cheval* and *Troupes à Pied*, both 1977; *Les Cuirassiers*, 1978.

Charrié, P. *Drapeaux et Etandards de la Révolution de de l'Empire*, Paris 1982.

Chartrand, R. *Napoleon's Overseas Army*, London 1989.

— *Napoleon's Sea Soldiers*, London 1990.

Dickens, Admiral Sir D. *The Dress of the British Sailor*, London 1977.

Elting, Col. J.R. (ed.) *Military Uniforms in America*, Vol. II, San Rafael, California 1977.

Fosten, B. *Wellington's Heavy Cavalry*, London 1982.

— *Wellington's Infantry I & II*, London 1981–2.

— *Wellington's Light Cavalry*, London 1982.

Grouvel, Vicomte *Les Corps de Troupes de l'Emigration Française 1789-1815*, Paris 1957.

Haswell Miller, A.E., & Dawnay, N.P. *Military Drawings and Paintings in the Royal Collection*, London 1966-70.

Haythornthwaite, P.J. *Austrian Army of the Napoleonic Wars, I Infantry, II Cavalry*, London 1986.

— *Austrian Specialist Troops of the Napoleonic Wars*, London 1990.

— *Napoleon's Guard Infantry, I*, London 1984.

— *Napoleon's Light Infantry*, London 1983.

— *Napoleon's Line Infantry*, London 1983.

— *Napoleon's Specialist Troops*, London 1988.

— *Nelson's Navy*, London 1993.

— *Russian Army of the Napoleonic Wars*, London 1987.

— *Uniforms of the Retreat from Moscow*, Poole 1976 (reprinted as *Uniforms of Napoleon's Russian Campaign*, London 1995).

— *Weapons and Equipment of the Napoleonic Wars*, Poole 1979.

Haythornthwaite, P.J., Cassin-Scott, J, & Fabb, J. *Uniforms of the Napoleonic Wars*, Poole 1973.

Hofschröer, P. *Hanoverian Army of the Napoleonic Wars*, London 1989.

— *Prussian Cavalry of the Napoleonic Wars: I 1792–1807*, London 1985.

— *Prussian Light Infantry 1792–1815*, London 1984.

— *Prussian Line Infantry 1792–1815*, London 1984.

Jarrett, D. *British Naval Dress*, London 1960.

Kannik, P. *Military Uniforms of the World*, Poole 1968.

Knötel, R. *Uniformkunde* (series of plates).

Knötel, R. & H., & Sieg, H. *Handbuch der Uniformkunde*, Hamburg 1937, reprinted 1964; English edition entitled *Uniforms of the World*, trans. R.G. Ball, London 1980.

Lackouque, H., & Blanckaert, G. *Les Drapeaux de la Garde Nationale de Paris en 1789*, Paris 1947.

Lawson, C.C.P. *History of the Uniforms of the British Army*, Vol. III London 1961, IV London 1966, V London 1967.

Linder, K. *Wojsko Polskie*, Warsaw 1964.

Malibran, H. *Guide à l'usage des Artistes et des Costumiers...des Uniformes de l'Armée française de 1780 à 1848*, Paris 1904–07, reprinted Krefeld 1972.

Martin, P. *Der Bunte Rock*, Stuttgart 1963; English edition entitled *European Military Uniforms*, London 1967.

— *Soldaten im Bunten Rock: Die französische Armee 1789–1807*, Stuttgart 1969.

Müller, H., & Kunter, F. *Europäische Helme aus der Sammlung des Museums für Deutsche Geschichte, Militärverlag der D.D.R.*, 1971.

Mollo, B. *Uniforms of the Imperial Russian Army*, Poole 1979.

Mollo, J. *Military Fashion*, London 1972.

— *Uniforms of the Royal Navy during the Napoleonic Wars*, London 1965.

Nicholson, Lt.Col. J.B.R. *Military Uniforms*, London 1973.

Ortenburg, G. *Preussische Husarenbilder um 1791*, Copenhagen 1976.

Ottenfeld, R. von, & Teuber, O. *Die Osterreichische Armee*, Vienna 1895.

Over, K. *Flags and Standards of the Napoleonic Wars*, London 1976.

Pivka, O. von *Napoleon's German Allies (4): Bavaria*, London 1980.

— *Napoleon's German Allies (5): Hessen-Darmstadt & Hessen-Kassel*, London 1982.

'Rigo' (A.Rigondaud) *Le Plumet* (series of plates).

Robson, B. *Swords of the British Army*, London 1975.

Rousselot, L. *L'Armée Française* (series of plates).

Rowlandson, T. *Loyal Volunteers of London and Environs*, London 1798–99.

Strachan, H. *British Military Uniforms 1768–96*, London 1975.

Wagner, E. *Cut and Thrust Weapons*, Prague & London 1967.

Wise, T. *Military Flags of the World 1618–1900*, Poole 1977.

Zweguintzow, W. *Drapeaux et Etandards de l'Armée Russe, XVIe Siècle à 1914*, Paris 1964.

Periodicals in which relevant information may be found include the *Journal of the Society for Army Historical Research, Carnet de la Sabretache, Gazette des Uniformes* (later *Uniformes*), and *Tradition*; *The British Military Library or Journal* (1798–1801) is an interesting contemporary source.